Critical Acclaim for *The Penny Pincher's Passport to Luxury Travel*

"This book delivers on its promise-indispensible, hard-earned knowledge on how to get more luxury and value in your travels."

—Joseph DiGiovanna, American Airlines

"This is one book that I can honestly say I wish I had written. It's a wonderful approach to the best kind of information anyone needs when they are traveling."

—Randy Petersen, editor and publisher, *InsideFlyer*

"As a former airline employee for twenty eight years, I feel this book will benefit any traveler and help them get the most luxury for their dollar."

—Stephanie Thomas, bookstore owner

"*The Penny Pincher's Passport* provides the reader with the experience needed to obtain added value and quality in their travels, whether business or vacation. It is extremely informative and is a small investment towards potentially great rewards."

—Clifford J. Naéole, Cultural Advisor,
The Ritz-Carlton Kapalua

"I thought I knew it all until I read this book—a must-read for every traveler."

— *Inside Flyer*

"For the penny pincher with a taste for luxury, here's a book to study and absorb."

—*San Francisco Examiner*

"It's rare that I feel compelled to recommend a travel book, but I can't resist talking about *The Penny Pincher's Passport to Luxury Travel*."

—*Rochester Democrat and Chronicle*

"Anyone with champagne tastes and beer budget is sure to appreciate this very wise guidebook."

—*Chicago Tribune*

Other Travelers' Tales Books

Country and Regional Guides

America, Australia, Brazil, France, India, Ireland, Italy, Japan, Mexico, Nepal, Spain, Thailand; Grand Canyon, Hawaii, Hong Kong, Paris, and San Francisco

Women's Travel

A Woman's Path, A Woman's Passion for Travel A Woman's World, Women in the Wild, A Mother's World, Safety and Security for Women Who Travel, Gutsy Women, Gutsy Mamas

Body & Soul

The Ultimate Journey, The Road Within, Love & Romance, Food, The Fearless Diner, The Gift of Travel

Special Interest

The Gift of Rivers, Danger!, Testosterone Planet, Shitting Pretty, There's No Toilet Paper on the Road Less Traveled, The Penny Pincher's Passport to Luxury Travel, The Fearless Shopper, The Gift of Birds, A Dog's World, Family Travel

Footsteps

Kite Strings of the Southern Cross, The Sword of Heaven, Storm

Travelers' Tales Guides

The PENNY PINCHER'S PASSPORT *to* *Luxury Travel*

TRAVELERS' TALES GUIDES

The PENNY PINCHER'S PASSPORT to Luxury Travel

JOEL L. WIDZER

TRAVELERS' TALES
SAN FRANCISCO

The Penny Pincher's Passport to Luxury Travel:
The Art of Cultivating Preferred Customer Status
By Joel L. Widzer

Copyright © 1999 Joel L. Widzer. All rights reserved.

Travelers' Tales and Travelers' Tales Guides are trademarks of
Travelers' Tales, Inc., 330 Townsend, Suite 208, San Francisco, California 94107.
www.travelerstales.com

Art direction by Kathryn Heflin
Cover design by Susan Bailey *Interior design by Patty Holden*
Cover and interior illustrations by © Michael Surles, watercolor painting
Page layout by Patty Holden, using the fonts Berkeley, Copperplate, Savoye, and Birch

Distributed by Publishers Group West, 1700 Fourth Street, Berkeley, CA 94710.

Library of Congress Cataloging-in-Publication Data
Widzer, Joel L.
The penny pincher's passport to luxury travel: the art of cultivating preferred customer status/by Joel L. Widzer—1st ed.
p. cm.
Includes bibliographical references
ISBN 1-885211-31-7
1. Travel—Guidebooks. I. Title
G153.4.W334 1999
910'.2'02—dc21 99-12211
CIP

First Edition
Printed in the United States of America
10 9 8 7 6 5 4 3 2

Afoot and light-hearted I take
to the open road,

Healthy, free, the world before me,

The long brown path before me leading
wherever I choose.

—Walt Whitman (1819–1892)

To Brittany:
Follow the passion of your Dreams

Table of Contents

1

Your Passport to Luxury

Traveling Like the Rich and Famous

The First Time I Saw Paris

My enduring love for luxury travel began the first time I saw Paris. The comfort and ease of my first class transatlantic flight had enabled me to arrive in that magical city relaxed and refreshed. But nothing prepared me for what I saw when I entered my elegant suite on the top floor of the fashionable, five-star Prince de Galles Hotel.

It was as if I had entered another world, a world of timeless beauty and unparalleled luxury. The floor I stood upon was sparkling marble; the plush fabrics of the furnishings were soft and inviting. Fresh, fragrant flowers in a crystal vase adorned a table that stood before a grand picture window. And through that window, regal and magnificent, was the Eiffel Tower.

From the moment I opened that door to the world of first class luxury travel, I vowed never to turn back. I have since traveled to more than twenty countries, on more than 500 first class flights, and to the finest five-star hotels known to the world. Now I can open those doors for you. *The Penny Pincher's Passport to Luxury Travel* is the first book to reveal the hidden secrets of how to access a world of first class travel, impeccable service, and preferred customer status—all at a fraction of the usual cost and regardless of your level of travel experience.

Through easy, step-by-step instructions and advice, you will learn how to obtain first class airline seats, the best hotel rooms, and the finest luxury rental cars—without having to spend a fortune. You will gain insight into the benefits of traveling against the grain, learn how to transform travel misfortunes into fortune, and understand how to spend travel dollars wisely. And you will discover the importance of building long-term, loyal relationships with travel companies, learn how to invest your tips wisely, and reap the rewards of researching your travel plans.

LUXURY TRAVEL: NO LONGER JUST FOR THE PRIVILEGED FEW

Along the journey of this book you will meet a few interesting individuals with whom I have had the opportunity to work first hand to help them secure a first class travel experience. These people are not wealthy; they have varied backgrounds and income levels, just like you. Their stories of achieving first class travel experiences at discount prices will help you see how easy it is to apply the fundamental principles of this book.

Each of these individuals fits into categories of travelers that I would define as frequent, moderate, occasional, or infrequent travelers. At the end of this chapter, you will see a chart that defines each category of traveler, along with annual travel budgets for each category. The budgets will give you an approximate yet realistic idea of how much you can expect to spend every year on travel for a first class experience; however, your actual costs will vary in accordance with the destinations you choose, the number of people in your family, and prevailing economic conditions.

You are going to meet Robert and Cindy, who are occasional travelers. They are a young couple in their late thirties with three children, two in high school and one in her first year of college. Robert and Cindy were married and had children when they were very young, and Cindy just received her college degree. Until recently they were not able to put any money aside for what they considered to be unnecessary activities like travel. However, it has always been their dream to take a second honeymoon, and you will see how they were able to enjoy a romantic and luxurious one-week trip to Bali on a tight budget of only $2,500.

Another couple, Mark and Donna, are what I would call infrequent travelers. They were able to take their two children on a wonderful seven-day family vacation to Disney World while staying well within their budget of $2,750. This budget included the cost of tickets to Disney World, which was $955 for the week. With the remaining $1,795, this family of four was able to fly first class at coach prices from Orange County, California to Orlando, Florida and stay in a spacious hotel suite for the same price as a small room.

Then you'll meet Lance, a single man in his thirties with a good job and a passion for first class travel. I would consider him a moderate traveler. The luxury travel bug bit Lance shortly after graduating from college, when his job gave him the opportunity to travel the world in the grandest style possible. He stayed at the finest hotels and flew worldwide in a private 727 and on commercial flights, but always in first class. However, when his assignment ended he came back to reality. Facing a puzzling dilemma, Lance, who was very thrifty, did not like to spend much of his own money on travel. However, after traveling in such a luxurious manner he did not want to settle for cramped coach seats and second-rate hotels. You will learn how Lance solved his dilemma and still travels in luxury while staying within his annual travel budget of $6,000.

After a lifetime of hard work, Ed and Carol, a retired couple in their sixties, feel that now is the time for them to see the world and pursue their love of travel. Like Lance, they are moderate travelers. However, Ed has some medical concerns, and when he travels he needs to be extra careful in securing his comfort. Ed and Carol also need to pay attention to their budget, since they are on a fixed income and could experience unexpected medical costs at any time. Working with Ed and Carol, I was able to help them satisfy their need for comfort while staying within their annual travel budget of $15,000.

Carl and Mary are your typical empty nesters who enjoy traveling now that their children are out of the house. Carl travels frequently for business, but would usually settle for coach airline seats, low frills hotels, and compact rental cars—until I showed him how to use the frequency of his travels to his advantage. Now he always travels in luxury, not only for business, but also for his personal travels with his wife Mary. Although Mary is an infrequent traveler, she has been able to benefit from Carl's frequent travels. Now both enjoy the comforts of first class travel while spending about $5,000 annually.

You will be introduced to Richard and Kathy, who live in the Midwest with their three children. Richard and Kathy are very involved in their children's activities; however, once a year they take time for themselves with a 10-day Caribbean cruise. Before I worked with Richard and Kathy, they were on a very tight budget of $3,500 and booked all their cruise arrangements through a travel agent. Now they make all their bookings themselves. Consequently, they enjoy a first class flight to their port destination and an upgraded cabin on the cruise ship. And the price of this enhanced travel experience? It's more than a thousand dollars cheaper than the cruise they used to book through a travel agent. With this extra savings they have been able to take another vacation with their children. This is not to say that it's a bad idea to use travel agents. Although I have found it more advantageous to book my own travel, there are many travel agents who are extremely knowledgeable about the travel marketplace, who can be very adept at helping you secure luxury travels at a discount, and who can be a valuable resource for all your travel needs. Later in this book I will discuss what to look for in a travel agent who will go the extra mile for you.

Throughout this book you will meet many other people who have enjoyed luxury travels at a discount. And of course, you will read about my own luxury travels throughout the world. I am a frequent traveler, and on average, approximately 60% of my travel is business related. With the exception of a few overseas flight segments that were in business class, all of my air travels since 1991 have been in first class. I fly over 100,000 air miles per year in first class and stay at the plushest hotels in the world—without breaking the bank. For instance, in 1996 I flew 125,000 air miles, which consisted of over 35 round trips and included three overseas trips—all in first class and for less than a total of $8,500. That is an average of $242 per round trip or .068 cents per mile flown. During that same year I spent 42 nights in hotel rooms for a total cost of $5,250. In 1997 I flew over 30 round trips, including four overseas trips, for a total of 107,000 miles and at a cost of $10,436. That year I spent 31 nights in hotels for a total of $4,265. By the end of 1998, I had flown at least 100,000 miles at a cost of $8,900.

Before we explore in detail the techniques for achieving first class travel at a discount, I'd like to discuss a factor that is crucial to having a truly satisfying travel experience, regardless of where or why you travel.

EXCEPTIONAL SERVICE: A HABIT YOU WON'T WANT TO BREAK

Memorable settings like my suite at the Prince de Galles Hotel in Paris are certainly an important aspect to any luxury travel experience. When you enter the lobby of a five-star hotel, your eyes will inform you. You'll see the marble floors and plush carpets, the sumptuously upholstered furnishings and white-gloved doormen. But amidst all the tangible trappings of luxury, it is the quality of service you receive from the staff of any travel company that can make or break your travel experience. When you receive impeccable service, you will step into a world that you thought was reserved for the rich and famous. You will know what it's like to feel welcomed, appreciated, and distinctly special when polished first class hotels and other travel companies go out of their way to make sure every little detail of your experience is flawless.

Although the best service will not add to your travel bill, it will greatly increase the rewards of traveling. Unfortunately, too many people feel that they either do not deserve or cannot afford to be pampered. This book will shift that perspective and give you the opportunity to experience, firsthand, pampered luxury travel—a habit you won't want to break.

WHAT IS EXCEPTIONAL SERVICE?

Understanding what defines exceptional service is imperative to a fully-realized luxury travel experience. If you lack a clear idea of what exceptional service is, you will neither grasp the full benefits of luxury travel nor be motivated enough to make it a priority.

Exceptional service is what companies provide when they take complete responsibility for and are accountable to their customer's needs. Their goal is to insure that the customer experiences total satisfaction with the product or services they offer. A company that provides exceptional service is a company that strives to set the standard in their industry for quality and believes that the customer is king and queen. In addition, it is a company that makes it a fundamental principle to maintain customer satisfaction by encouraging feedback from customers and adjusting company policy and strategies according to their customers' needs.

As a consumer, you experience exceptional service when a company or an employee of a company possesses a keen ability to anticipate your needs and responds with accommodating actions that will enrich your comfort. Service employees who are sensitive to a customer's needs know not only when to offer services, but also know when not to. Exceptional service also involves a perceptive attention to details and a knowledge that often it is the small things that matter most. Most importantly, it incorporates a "can-do" attitude in which the customer is of foremost concern and treated with priority.

While traveling in Asia, I noticed the attentiveness of the staff members in the restaurants. When entering a restaurant you instantly feel the observant yet understated attention of the employees. A polite and gracious host immediately greets you and escorts you to your table. When you sit down, your waiter is at your side, unfolding your napkin and welcoming you to the restaurant. He takes your order for beverages and swiftly brings them to you. Whenever you take a drink of water, he quickly refills your glass. And as soon as you have finished your meal, he is ready to clear your table. With an acute sensitivity to your needs, your waiter is available at all times without being intrusive.

Regardless of how busy these restaurants are, the employees make you feel as if you are the only person in the restaurant. I remember once glancing over at a man who had just pulled a cigarette from his pocket and immediately had five lighters at his disposal. On one occasion I asked a waiter why the staff was so motivated and in sync with the customer's needs. He replied, "If we were not, our customers would go elsewhere."

That statement made me think how wonderful a time it is to be a consumer. With the emergence of the global economy, competition has become amazingly fierce, especially in the service sector. Today's consumers have a substantial number of choices and a vast selection of companies from which to choose when deciding to spend money. Fortunately, if a business fails to meet your needs, a more obliging competitor will be happy to win your business.

Successful companies who wish to compete in today's global economy must work to meet the needs of their customers by providing high-quality service. This is what provides travelers the opportunity to take advantage of, but not exploit, competition. Any attempts to exploit a company's quest for providing top quality service will eventually result in unwillingness by that company to continue extending their warmth and courtesy.

It is also important to remember that although businesses want to provide for their customers' needs, they cannot do so to the detriment of the business. All companies need to consider the profitability of their operation. Therefore, it is important to learn what accommodations and exceptions are feasible for a company to make. This concept will be discussed in greater detail in a later chapter.

Quality Service Means Taking Responsibility and Going the Extra Mile

The employees of the Ritz-Carlton Hotels do an excellent job in taking responsibility for problems and acting with initiative. Displayed throughout the workers' area in the Ritz-Carlton Hotels are signs reminding employees to take responsibility for their guests' needs. It is this consistent sense of responsibility on the part of employees that provides the guests of the Ritz-Carlton Hotels with exceptional service.

When I was a guest of the Ritz-Carlton in Hong Kong, I noticed that along the side of my bed there was a conspicuous button marked "service." Being curious and even a little skeptical that someone would actually respond if I pushed the button, I pushed it. Within a few short minutes, a valet appeared at my door. Embarrassed by his rapid and obviously earnest response, I asked if I could have a pair of slacks pressed. He told me that it was Sunday and the cleaning service did not operate on Sundays; however, he would do his best to accommodate me. Within thirty minutes he returned with my freshly pressed slacks. Clearly, he had gone out of his way to give me exceptional service, and for that I gave him a generous tip. This is a fine example of the type of service you should expect as a luxury traveler.

My experience at a particular Four Seasons Hotel is another example of exceptional service. On one occasion, I was traveling with my two dogs, and when making my reservations, I requested that I be allowed to bring them to the hotel with me. To my surprise, a few days prior to my arrival, the hotel called me to ask about the size of the dogs, their favorite treats, and their names. And when I arrived at my room, the hotel had prepared a special area for my dogs with their own beds, treats, and special bowls imprinted with their names! I believe that this is going the extra mile.

Don't Settle for Less than the Best

While dining at the Ritz-Carlton Kapalua in Hawai'i with my wife, I learned how important it is to choose only travel companies that make exceptional service a high priority. About ten minutes after we sat down at our table, an older gentleman who from outward appearances seemed to be very wealthy sat at a table adjacent to ours, accompanied by a well-dressed young woman. The waiter, who was responsible for both tables, took one look at the other couple and completely neglected my wife and me for the remainder of our meal while showering them with impeccable service. When their wine glasses were empty, the waiter rushed to refill them, and in the meantime my wife's glass remained unfilled. When the other man's female companion returned to their table after a brief absence, the waiter raced across the room to assist her with her chair. Yet we sat needlessly long with our dinner plates needing to be cleared. It took so long for us to get our waiter's attention that we decided not to wait for dessert, and left the restaurant without leaving a tip for the waiter.

Apparently our dissatisfaction was communicated to the hotel's Food and Beverage Manager, who called our room to express his concern. After discussing our poor service, he apologized profusely and offered to make amends. When I mentioned that we were unable to order dessert, he offered us complimentary desserts of our choice. Within two minutes, a room service waiter delivered them to our room, and the Food and Beverage Manager paid for our entire meal that evening.

Once you understand what quality service is, you should

not accept anything less. When you appreciate the impact that service has on your travel experiences you know why you should only spend your travel dollars on companies that make it a habit to offer quality service. This principle will be discussed in greater detail later in this book. Undoubtedly, things will go wrong on occasion, no matter what kind of travel company you choose as a consumer. However, if my wife and I had dined at a hotel that was accustomed to offering a lower level of service, the Food and Beverage Manager probably would not have taken an interest in or responsibility for our dissatisfaction. Consequently, part of our travel experience would have been disappointing.

LET SMART SERVICE EMPLOYEES BRING OUT THE BEST IN YOU

What my wife and I observed in the dining room of the Ritz-Carlton Kapalua is not uncommon. Often, waiters and other service personnel offer the rich and famous a discriminatory level of lavish service because of a preconceived notion that wealthy clientele will tip more generously than the rest of us. However, savvy workers know that this is often not the case. Having worked my way through college in service sector jobs, I learned first hand that people of average income are usually better tippers. As a valet at a Malibu, California beachfront restaurant, I constantly received higher tips from the drivers of average cars, whereas the drivers of luxury cars would often tip a pittance or nothing at all. I still find this observation to hold true, as evidenced by what I see every Saturday when I get my car washed. I bought my car from a dealer who offers free Saturday car washes to owners of this type of vehicle. Each Saturday the dealer fills the reception room with pastries, bagels, doughnuts, coffee, and juices. Human nature being what it is, car owners happily partake in the free food and services. However, when the attendants pull up with their nicely washed car, most of the owners who paid in excess of $50,000 for their vehicles do not even have the courtesy to tip one dollar for this gracious service.

Another good example of this tendency to prejudge customers comes from a friend of mine who was shopping for a Porsche in Beverly Hills. On that particular day, he was wearing a t-shirt and a pair of jeans. When he first walked onto the lot, he was shunned by all the salespeople except for one astute salesperson who treated my friend graciously and courteously. The salesman made such an impression on my friend that he bought a Porsche that same day, in cash and at list price. The other salespeople were dismayed, and more to the point, without a sale.

In any event, those employees who prejudge customers based solely on outward appearances are not the kind of employees you want serving your needs. You want to find the personnel who will readily and genuinely provide quality service to you and go the extra mile, whether your travel bill amounts to a dime or a hundred dollars. And when you are the recipient of good service, you have an added responsibility to treat others how you would like to be treated. It is your responsibility not to take advantage of service industry employees in your pursuit of fine service. Remember that these people will go the extra mile for you, but you must show respect and appreciation for their hard work and most importantly, do not treat them like servants. I guarantee you will learn how to travel to a five-star resort and receive preferential treatment; however, when receiving this fine service you should be respectful and reciprocate. In the chapter on tipping, you will see how you can reward these individuals and in return receive treatment fit for a king.

Our everyday lives are typically involved with serving others. If you are an employee, you are most likely serving your supervisor and customers. If you are a homemaker, you are probably serving the needs of your family. If you are a business traveler, your journeys are strenuous enough with long daily meetings in a new city each day, along with being away from the comforts of family and home. We all work hard in whatever field of endeavor we have chosen, and so it is vital to reward ourselves whenever we have the opportunity. I have found luxury travel to be a well-deserved reward for hard work.

Regardless of what you do or what your reasons are for traveling, your journeys away can provide you with the opportunity to take a luxurious break from the stresses of daily life. This is your time to pamper yourself and to enjoy your sensual surroundings. So experience the highest level of quality service by seeking out the quality companies that make it their mission to give all of their customers preferential treatment.

Key Points

- ➢ Believe you deserve nothing but the best, regardless of your travel budget or frequency of travel.
- ➢ Cultivate an understanding of and appreciation for high quality service; it can make or break your trip.
- ➢ Seek out those who readily and genuinely offer quality service.
- ➢ Respect and reward those who do offer good service.

Traveling in Luxury: *You, Too, Can Afford It!*

	AIRLINE	HOTEL	CAR RENTAL	STRATEGY
FREQUENT TRAVELER 10+ round trips or 50,000+ miles 30+ flight segments 10+ hotel nights 10+ car rentals Air budget \$3,000–\$8,500 Hotel budget \$750–\$1,500 Car budget \$200–\$350 Combined \$4,700–\$10,350	Top elite level in most airline frequent flyer programs	Top elite level in most hotel frequent guest programs	Top preferred status with major car rental companies	Loyalty Knowledge of travel companies Leverage and automatic upgrades due to top level Elite Status Skillful use of key contacts Call travel companies directly for bookings Flexibility of dates and times
MODERATE TRAVELER 5–10 round trips or 20,000–50,000 miles 20–40 flight segments 5–10 hotel nights 5–10 car rentals Air budget \$1,050–\$5,500 Hotel \$500–\$1,000 Car budget \$100–\$175 Combined \$2,150–\$6,675	Mid level elite status in most airline frequent flyer programs	Preferred status with most major hotel frequent guest programs	Preferred status in most car rental programs	Loyalty Knowledge of travel companies Skillful use of key contacts Leverage and upgrades due to Elite Status Call travel companies directly for bookings Earn free Upgrade Certificates through miles flown and ancillary programs Flexibility of dates and times

	AIRLINE	HOTEL	CAR RENTAL	STRATEGY
OCCASIONAL TRAVELER 3–5 Round Trips or 5–20,000 miles 5–20 Flight segments 2–5 Hotel nights 1–5 Car rentals Air budget $600–$1,450 Hotel Budget $200–$500 Car Budget $25–$199 Combined $925–$2,149	First tier elite status with most airline frequent flyer programs	First tier elite status with most hotel frequent guest programs	Preferred status in most car rental programs	Loyalty Knowledge of travel companies Leverage due to Minimum Elite Status Continue to build partnerships with select travel companies Call travel companies directly for bookings Earn free Upgrade Certificates through miles flown and ancillary programs and purchase upgrades at nominal cost when necessary High flexibility of dates and times
INFREQUENT TRAVELER 1–2 Round Trips or 1-5,000 miles 1–4 Flight segments 1–2 Hotel nights 1–2 Car rentals Air budget $199–$299 Hotel Budget $75–$150 Car Budget $50 Combined $499	Preferred customer status	Preferred customer status	Membership in preferred car rental program	Careful travel planning, Call travel companies directly for bookings Maximum flexibility; non-peak, off-season travel Use of ancillary miles and/or purchase of upgrade certificates at nominal cost Leveraging partnerships; promise of continued future loyalty

These figures are based on the lowest available '98 rates and fares and travel during off-peak and off-season times. Rates and fares can be higher or lower depending on the economy and the specific pattern of travel.

2

A Lifetime of Loyalty

Reaping the Rewards of Leverage

A close friend of mine, who flies over 200,000 miles a year on one particular airline, attempted to cash in his frequent flyer miles to fly five of his family members to Hawaii during the December holidays. At first, he went through the usual channels of calling the airline's reservation line. Anyone who has ever wanted to secure first class seats during this busy time of the year knows how difficult it is to find just one seat available, even if you are willing to pay full price. Trading in miles for tickets during the Christmas holidays is virtually impossible, even if you try to reserve them a year in advance. Not surprisingly, my friend was told that there was not a single seat available, let alone five, until the following April. Naturally, he was disappointed. Nevertheless, he decided to call the Vice President of Marketing for this airline. He simply said that because he was a loyal passenger who flew only on that one airline, he would appreciate anything he could do to secure five tickets for the dates in question. Suddenly, five "nonexistent" first class tickets to Hawaii became available.

My friend was able to acquire these highly sought-after seats for one very important reason: he was a steadfastly loyal customer to that one airline.

Loyalty is the Most Essential Strategy For Those Who Travel First class and Pay Coach Prices

Since I have begun flying, 97% of my flights have been flown on one particular airline. Consequently, I have become a Million Miler, which means I have accrued over one million miles in my frequent flyer account with that airline. Because of my steadfast loyalty to one airline, I am privy to many special concessions and benefits. And although I always pay the most discounted fares, I am automatically upgraded to first class—every time. When I fly overseas, I usually receive a two-class upgrade, from coach to first class, and I am provided entrée to luxurious first class lounges. Whenever I need an exception to a rule or restriction, my loyalty has given me the leverage to supersede this airline's strictest rules.

Promoting Loyalty is a Powerful Incentive

Promoting loyalty has become a powerful incentive for today's businesses, and for this simple reason: 80% of most companies' revenues are generated from 20% of their customers.

Today's competitive market environment has created a windfall of opportunity for the customer whose consumer loyalty has become an omnipotent bargaining chip. Here's how customer loyalty works in any business: consumers respond to incentives. Businesses know this and promote loyalty by offering incentives to their most loyal customers. Throughout the history of marketing, promoting customer loyalty has been an enduring marketing objective of businesses.

Why is your loyalty so important to a business? Because companies know it is far less expensive to maintain happy customers than to continuously search for new ones. It costs hundreds of dollars to attract a new customer; therefore, companies want their customers to remain loyal. Furthermore, companies know that customer retention is key to their growth and profitability. A 1998 *Harvard Business Review* article reported that increasing a customer's retention rate by only 5% could increase the value of the average customer by as much as 100%. Further studies indicated that the average company with a customer retention rate of 95% would grow 50% faster than a company with a 90% retention rate. Additionally, a 5% increase in retention increased company profits by 125%. The link between the forces of loyalty and profitability are clear.

Companies clearly understand that loyal customers stimulate their business and initiate a series of economic benefits to the company. When customers are loyal, a company's revenues and market share will grow, building repeat and referral customers. That is why if a company is threatened with the loss of an established loyal customer, it will make concessions to keep that customer. Those concessions translate into a tremendously lucrative tool for knowledgeable consumers.

If You Build a Loyal Partnership, Rewards Will Come

When you establish a loyal customer relationship with a business, you are in essence building a mutually beneficial partnership with that business. Building a partnership is what allows you, the consumer, to use your loyalty as a valuable investment. This investment pays huge dividends and greatly enhances the manner in which these companies treat you. Remember, your repeat business has value to even the biggest companies, no matter how little or how much you spend. After all, the long term promise of even the modest amount of income your business brings to a company is worth a great deal, especially when multiplied by the hundreds of thousands of other loyal customers who are just like you. Think about it: if you were the CEO of a major airline, wouldn't you feel secure knowing that hundreds of thousands of people will continue to spend even a few hundred dollars flying your airline every year?

These days, almost all types of businesses promote and track the loyalty of their customers through incentive programs that offer preferential services, prices, and rewards to their most loyal customers. A major force in retailing, Neiman Marcus, offers the In Circle program in which shoppers can earn rewards ranging from lavish trips to New York City, Hawaii, and New Zealand to ten hours of air service on a private Learjet or a 1999 Jaguar XJ8—just by being a loyal customer. Hallmark Card stores recently launched a frequent purchaser program with their Hallmark Customer Card, which gives customers opportunities to earn awards and gifts. The three dominant long distance telephone companies, AT&T, MCI, and Sprint, are going to extreme lengths to promote loyalty among their current customers. They offer incentives such as discounts, free connect charges, free Internet access, paging, cellular communication, and satellite television. Incidentally, AT&T and Sprint also have reward programs in which members earn points that can be redeemed as airline tickets and discounts, gift certificates, or free long distance calling. Even small businesses compete for loyal customers by offering incentives. After ten purchases, your neighborhood car wash might offer you a free car wash, and your corner yogurt store might give you a free yogurt.

Even if a particular company doesn't have an organized incentive program, you can find ways to profit from your loyal consumerism. Here's how I used my customer loyalty to my advantage while shopping for a television at Circuit City, a West Coast electronics retailer. I approached the sales manager and told him that I'd previously purchased a washer and dryer, refrigerator, and other smaller items from this chain. He looked up my customer record, which detailed my past purchases as far back as a television I bought five years ago in another state. Because of my long-term, loyal customer history, he offered me the television for only $10 above cost. One year later, I still have not seen the same model television at a lower price.

Loyalty can pay off for even your smallest purchases. Each morning I venture to my local Starbucks coffee store for a café latte. With the increased popularity of gourmet coffee, the line at Starbucks is a long one indeed. However, due to my faithful patronage, the employees at Starbucks start preparing my coffee as soon as they see me entering the store, thereby saving me the inconvenience of having to wait in line.

In today's global economy, competition is fierce, and any smart business recognizes the value of a loyal customer. Savvy consumers are aware of the benefits of building loyal relationships with astute companies. As a result, both the consumer and the companies profit in a win-win situation.

Quick Review

- Successful businesses seek out and reward loyal customers.
- Businesses offer attractive incentives to promote your loyalty.

- Build a partnership with a company by being a loyal customer, and become privy to valuable amenities.
- Customer loyalty is a win-win situation for you and the company with which you do business.

How the Travel Industry Cultivates Loyal Customers

The travel industry zealously subscribes to the loyalty principle, using frequent-user programs to promote and track the repeat business of their customers and offering special incentives to the most loyal. Computer technology has made it much easier for travel industry companies to track a customer's history. By viewing a frequent flyer's history, an airline knows who its loyal passengers are. In return for their loyalty, passengers obtain special upgrade opportunities, discounted fares, preferred seating, and a greater opportunity to build additional account miles. Similarly, most hotels track their guests' previous stays and provide frequent guests with upgraded rooms for no extra cost or at discounted prices, special incentives during off-peak times, and enhanced levels of service. And recently, many car rental companies have initiated frequent renter programs that provide renters with opportunities to receive free upgraded cars and free car rentals.

Understanding the importance that travel companies place on customer loyalty is your opportunity to profit as a consumer. It is essential that you establish a history of loyalty with select travel companies in order to consistently obtain preferential treatment and services that are normally reserved for those who pay first class prices. Therefore, begin to build partnerships with quality travel companies.

This will be the cornerstone of your strategy of traveling first class at coach prices.

WHY YOUR LOYALTY IS MORE IMPORTANT TO AN AIRLINE THAN WITH ANY OTHER TRAVEL PARTNER

In 1983 the airline industry became deregulated. The result of deregulation was that the airline industry evolved into a highly competitive business in which low airfares became the driving force behind the competition. Without allegiance or loyalty to any particular airline, passengers flocked to whichever airline had the lowest fares. Airfare wars ensued, creating an economic windfall for consumers. The airlines, however, racked up tremendous losses.

Faced with the choice of cutting expenses or going out of business, many airlines cut back on the services offered to their passengers. It also became essential for airlines to increase their revenues by increasing the number of passengers on board. But with the demise of such low-frills carriers as People Express, the airline industry also realized that passengers expected an adequate level of service as well as low fares.

In the past, the airlines could always count on a core group of business travelers. However, with more and more corporations cutting costs, a recent study from *The Wall Street Journal* concluded that only 47% of air traffic is generated from business travel. The result is that airlines are increasingly reliant on the average consumer.

In order for the airlines to maintain both competitive fares and a profit margin, they searched for an innovative means of competing for customers. To meet the demands of the flying public, the airlines needed to offer enhanced services to remain competitive, and most importantly, a means to maintain loyal customers.

Because of this fierce competition, the airlines will go to great lengths to court passenger loyalty. This has created an opportunity for anyone who wishes to travel first class and pay coach prices. Upgrading passengers to first class is a classic win-win situation for you and the airlines, who actually get more out of the deal than the chance to expand their base of loyal customers. When an airline upgrades a coach passenger to first class, they have the chance to sell that coach seat twice—once to the person who was upgraded to the first class seat that otherwise would have gone empty, and then to the person who ends up sitting in the coach seat.

FREQUENT FLYER PROGRAMS

In an effort to increase ticket sales and appeal to the average traveler, American Airlines introduced the first frequent flyer program in 1981. This was the dawn of a new era of rewarding loyal passengers.

Since 1981, frequent flyer programs have evolved into a commonplace component of a consumer's everyday life. The availability of frequent flyer miles is now so widespread that they have almost become our second national currency. Almost everyone is involved in some sort of program that earns airline mileage. Consumers can earn air miles from an ever-widening range of sources, from credit cards to long distance telephone calls to even paying their mortgages. And many people base their purchasing decisions on whether or not they will earn miles.

Frequent flyer programs have been a triumphant success for the airlines in helping them maintain a loyal base of customers. And in return, the airlines reward their loyal passengers by offering them enhanced services.

CHOOSE YOUR TRAVEL INDUSTRY PARTNERS WISELY

The first thing to consider in your plans to build a loyal customer history is the all-important question: Which companies should you choose as your travel industry partners? As this decision will have an impact on the quality of your travel experiences, you should choose your travel partners wisely. And since you are embarking on a long-term relationship with these companies, you will want to be selective. Carefully decide which companies will best meet your needs.

When choosing an airline partner, consider what air routes you are most likely to fly and from which airports. Keep in mind that although most major airlines fly to most major cities, some airlines might have a hub city that could be more convenient for you. Another factor to consider is the airline's code share agreements. A code share agreement is a sort of partnership that your chosen airline has with other airlines. This means you can fly to cities outside the route of your chosen airline on another carrier, but still have your chosen airline issue the ticket, enabling you to earn mileage on it as well. In any case, the most important consideration is to find out which airlines will provide you with the greatest flexibility and opportunity to reach the most cities.

One excellent program, which was initiated in May 1997, links multiple airline frequent flyer programs together to form what is called the Star Alliance. Currently, United, Lufthansa, Thai, Air Canada, SAS, Varig, Air New Zealand and Ansett Australia are part of this alliance. The Star Alliance offers travelers the opportunity to fly on any of the participating airlines and not only earn frequent flyer mileage on their chosen airline travel partner, but also earn mileage towards the so-called elite level of frequent flyer status on that airline. (Elite levels will be covered in detail in Chapter Five.) The Star Alliance allows you to travel the world on one seamless system. Travelers participating in the alliance receive benefits such as access to all the airlines' first class lounges worldwide, as well as coordinated reservations, flight schedules, and ticketing. Another key benefit is that if you have established an elite frequent flyer level with your chosen airline, you will receive the benefits of your elite status on any of the Alliance's participating airlines.

Programs like the Star Alliance are already a growing trend among air carriers. In the fall of 1998, American Airlines and British Airways, along with Canadian Airlines, Cathay Pacific, and Qantas, joined together to form the Oneworld Alliance. In addition, Swissair, Sabena, and Austrian Airlines have merged their frequent flyer programs into a program called Qualiflyer, to which they have recently added the following airlines: TAP Air Portugal, Turkish Airlines, AOM French Airlines, Crossair, Lauda Air, and Tyrolean Airways. And this is just the beginning. According to Randy Petersen of *InsideFlyer Magazine*, the future should hold the introduction of a "Universal Mileage Card." This card would replace individual program cards and unite various frequent flyer programs into one all-inclusive alliance.

These new alliances are an excellent opportunity for air travelers, because they virtually open the doors to the world. Even if your chosen airline does not fly to a given destination, you can fly on any other carrier within the alliance and still reap the rewards of customer loyalty. Therefore, when choosing an airline partner, you might want to ask if any of the carriers you're considering participates in this kind of program. If your chosen airline allows you the flexibility to fly on a number of other carriers while continuing to build on your customer history, you will have much more of an incentive to remain that airline's loyal customer.

In choosing hotels as travel partners, your strategy will be different in some respects from your strategy in choosing other travel partners. For example, competing airlines offer very similar fares and routes. In sharp contrast to this is the great disparity in rates between different hotels. This disparity can even be found within the same hotel chain, depending upon, among other factors, the specific hotel's geographical location. Therefore, your wisest strategy is to join a select number of frequent guest programs with hotel companies that you feel can best meet your specific needs. Be aware, however, that you do not want to spread your business among too many hotel chains. The actual number of frequent guest programs you join will depend upon the frequency of your travels. You will want to limit the number to an amount that will allow you to demonstrate a pattern of loyalty with each company. Like all other travel partners, hotels track the history of their guests, and the hotel guests who come back the most will be privy to the greatest number of enhanced services.

Be Assiduously Loyal to Your Travel Partners

I cannot emphasize enough the importance of adhering to this principle. By maintaining loyalty to one travel partner, you are more likely to achieve the most elite levels as a customer, giving you access to the greatest number of benefits. To maintain your loyalty, you will need to remain flexible. This principle is discussed in full detail later in the book. For now, keep in mind that your chosen travel partner might not always be the most convenient. This means that you might have to take a connecting flight rather than a non-stop flight or stay at a hotel that is five minutes away from your intended destination. Yet, you will find that your flexibility is well worth the effort when you are luxuriating in the finest travel experience imaginable.

Carl, the frequent business traveler whom we met in the first chapter, was spending his travel dollars on a potpourri of travel companies, thinking that this was the best way to save money. With five more business trips coming up, I persuaded him to re-think his travel strategy. We looked at his receipts for past trips and called several airlines and hotels to shop around for rates and fares. Surprisingly, he quickly saw that there was not a significant price difference among the various travel companies he used. He then chose the one airline that had the best service from his home city and with which he had had the best travel experiences. He also chose one hotel chain that would meet most of his needs. I then suggested that Carl call the airline and hotel chain (both the main hotel reservation number and each individual hotel property where he planned to stay) to let them know that he was shifting his business to them from now on. As a result, his preferred airline offered him elite level status in their frequent flyer program, which allows him free first class upgrade opportunities, and all five of the hotel properties upgraded him to a nice room. Carl is now a dedicated loyal traveler reaping some valuable benefits. (Incidentally, even if you are not a frequent traveler this technique will work for you. All you have to do is invest a little time to research your travel partners and call them to express your intended loyalty—and then follow through.)

In Chapters Five, Six, and Seven you will learn more ways you can cash in on your customer loyalty with airlines, hotels, and car rental companies.

A Few Last Words about Loyalty

Loyalty is an essential element of smart consumerism. When you establish a loyal history with a business, you will be privy to a cornucopia of benefits. As a loyal customer, you have power, and that power gives you leverage. Companies that understand the future of marketing will strive to cultivate your business. Fortunately for today's consumer, the products and services within most industries are very similar in nature. Therefore, competitive markets provide a broad range of options and choices for smart consumers. This is markedly true with travel industry companies. Maintain your loyalty to select travel companies and reap the rewards of luxury.

And remember, in addition to building a loyal history with travel partners, you can establish a history with virtually anyone with whom you do business. Almost all types of industries will reward loyalty.

Key Points

➢ ***Choose your travel partners wisely.***
It's in your best interest to build a long-term relationship with your travel industry partners, so choose these companies wisely and build a high level of loyalty.

➢ ***Reap the rewards of your loyalty.***
Your high level of loyalty will pay off with tremendous benefits and allow you to consistently travel first class and pay coach prices.

- ***Maintain the loyalty you have carefully built with your travel partners.***
  Even if it requires flexibility, your loyalty will pay off.

- ***Seek out all opportunities to build loyal customer relationships.***
  A wealth of benefits and amenities await those consumers who have the wisdom and patience to seek them out.

3

Your Travel Partners

Getting What You Pay For

On one trip to New York, I thought I would take advantage of a limousine service that was advertised in an airline in-flight magazine. The ad offered a low price for this limousine service from the airport into Manhattan, and I figured I would use it to get to my hotel. It sounded like a good deal—until I actually experienced the service. When I called in advance to arrange for the limousine, the phone operator confirmed my arrival flight number, the time, and date. However, when I arrived at the airport there was no suited driver waiting to whisk me away. Instead, I had to call the service again and wait 30 minutes for "car number 321" to arrive. This, my first clue, was strike one. When car number 321 finally arrived, it looked like it had been on a road trip with the gang from *Animal House*. Strike two! As I climbed into the car, the driver informed me that the air conditioning was broken—and this was in the middle of a hot and humid summer. Strike three, and you're out!

Bad things often come in three's, but in this case it was not over yet. En route to my hotel, the driver made a 20-minute detour to drop off his friend who was riding in the front seat (I had assumed at the time he was some kind of trainee driver).

When I arrived at the Ritz-Carlton in New York, I was so frustrated by this miserable experience that I refused to pay the driver. I told him that he could call his manager and I would talk to him, but I would not pay for such poor service. He did not even debate the issue with me. The bellman at the Ritz-Carlton, who assisted me with my bags, told me that a couple had arrived at the hotel the day before and had also refused to pay this same limo company because of the poor service. Their car (which was a different color than mine) had a broken air conditioner as well. We surmised that this must have been the company's ploy to save on gas.

PAY NOW OR PAY LATER

Occasionally you will find it necessary to pay a bit more for luxury. This concept is best supported by the caveat "pay now or pay later," and is abundantly illustrated by my so-called deal of a ride with that so-called limo company. While it is not the aim of this book to encourage you to spend extravagantly, you should know that on occasion you will find it necessary to spend a slight premium for quality. However, keep in mind that if you are willing to spend a little, you will get more than you ever dreamed possible. And remember that *your willingness to occasionally pay a bit more than rock bottom will ultimately save you money as well as stress.*

For example, according to a recent article in *The Wall Street Journal*, Southwest Airlines is able to achieve their high on-time status and low, low fares by having one of the highest bumped percentages of all airlines. Therefore, if you hope to get a decent seat (or any seat at all) on Southwest you will sometimes need to arrive long before the departure of your flight. Similarly, many low frills or start-up carriers do not have the extensive inventory of planes in their fleet that major carriers have. Consequently, if there is a mechanical malfunction it usually takes a low-frills or start-up carrier a long time to replace that plane. As a result, you the traveler could be stranded at the airport instead of traveling in a mode akin to the rich and famous. If, however, you had chosen one of the major carriers and perhaps, but not necessarily, paid just a bit more for your ticket, that carrier's more extensive supply of planes would usually enable them to roll out a new plane or place you on an alternate flight in a relatively short period of time. Therefore, the inconvenience to you would be minimized, and you would have a far greater chance of traveling in a preferential mode. Furthermore, it is less stressful when you can casually stroll on board a plane to your assigned seat and find ample overhead space for your carry-on luggage rather than wait in long lines and battle for space.

Don't Just Save Money; Spend it Wisely

When you are in need of medical care, you are most likely to seek out the highest level of care possible. After all, would you want an unskilled surgeon performing a triple bypass surgery on you or a loved one? Likewise when you wish to purchase the highest quality product or service, you are not likely to shop at a five and dime store. The same principle holds true for traveling. We learned in the last chapter the importance of doing business with quality companies.

If you seek the utmost in luxury travel, you will find that occasionally you will need to pay a modest premium. However, when you utilize the strategies discussed in this book you will not pay an excessive sum of money, and you will find that the added benefits of ultra luxurious travels will far exceed any additional amount of money you might pay. Most importantly, you will need to deal exclusively with companies that consistently offer superior service.

If you are, on occasion, faced with the prospect of paying a slight premium for the opportunity to travel in luxury, is it worth it? Absolutely. The philosophy of those who travel first class and pay coach prices is not only to save money, but also to spend it wisely in order to reap first class rewards. To understand this, you will need to consider the overall cost of travel and the impact your travels will have on your peace of mind. This means you should consider the actual costs of a trip from both a monetary as well as an emotional perspective. The monetary side is easy to understand: You want to get the most luxurious travel experience for the least amount of money. However, as you become a more experienced traveler you will find that the lowest price is not always the best deal. The emotional aspect of your trip affects your overall level of satisfaction and the ease in which you experience your travels. This brings to us back to the important concept of limiting your business to quality companies in order to receive quality service. Remember that every aspect of your trip can affect your overall experience.

Without a doubt, you will be able to find airfares that might save you $100 or a hotel room for 5% to 10% less; however, consider what other costs are associated with this savings. Will you have to arrive at the airport three hours early and fight a crowd of people vying for unreserved seats or at the very least wait in a long line to get a seat? Will the quality of service you receive be poor? Will you question the safety record of the air carrier? Will you be able to cash in your miles for only limited travel destinations? Will you be able to sleep in your hotel room at night when the bed is uncomfortable and the neighbors are noisy? Will you feel comfortable with the level of cleanliness in your room? Will you feel safe in the rental car you're driving? What happens if that car breaks down on you, en route to an important meeting or family outing?

To illustrate the distinctive rewards you will reap from doing business exclusively with quality travel companies, consider the difference between what you can receive from United Airlines versus Southwest Airlines. When flying United Airlines, you can usually have the advantage of paying the same low fare as Southwest, but unlike Southwest, United offers pre-assigned seating. On Southwest you will need to wait in a bothersome line to take your chances at winning the lottery of seats. Like United, Southwest Airlines does offer frequent flyer recognition; however, Southwest frequent flyers are restricted to the limited routes flown by that airline. In contrast, United Airlines provides worldwide coverage and the ability to fly on code-share routes. And the most important consideration of all to the readers of this book is that Southwest will not upgrade you to first class. Unlike United, Southwest does not have first class cabins.

As an analogy, consider for a moment the slew of discount stockbrokers who in the past few years have begun to offer low commission rates. Many of the people who flock to these discount brokers do receive those low commission rates; however, they also receive inferior service, poor execution rates, and the inability to reach a broker in a time-sensitive situation. Further, they soon discover that they are being nickeled and dimed for the smallest fees, like postage and handling. Although this book is not about the brokerage industry, this example aptly illustrates the point that sometimes when you think you are getting a lower price or a good deal, it might not be so good after all. We have all heard the saying, "if it sounds too good to be true, it probably is." *This is remarkably true in the travel industry.*

LUXURY OFTEN COSTS THE SAME OR EVEN LESS

While it is certainly worth it to pay a little more to have a pleasant and comfortable experience, the idea of this book is to *travel luxuriously and to save money.* Therefore, by doing a little research and by keeping your standards of quality high, you will find that you do not always have to pay more for luxury. In fact, occasionally a luxury rental car, a more upscale hotel room, and even a first class airline seat can actually cost you less than what you might pay for a low frills experience.

On a trip to the Big Island of Hawai'i, I booked a first class flight on Delta. Because Delta does not fly all the way to the Big Island, I flew on Delta to Oahu, and the Delta reservationist arranged a connecting flight for me from Oahu to the Big Island on Hawaiian Air. On my Delta ticket, the cost was split between the Delta portion and the Hawaiian Air portion. When I made my reservations, it didn't even occur to me that my Hawaiian Air flight might not have the same quality of service as Delta. However, my failure to make inquiries led to an unpleasant surprise. I found out, too late, that Hawaiian Air does not offer pre-assigned seating or first class on their inter-island flights. I found myself waiting in a long line at the Oahu Airport to board the Hawaiian Air plane in a cattle-like manner. Once I made my way on board the plane, I was constrained to the smallest airline seat I have ever sat in. And after the plane landed, it took me over twenty minutes to deplane. Determined not to repeat this experience on my return flight, I did my homework and called another inter-island airline, Aloha Air, which did offer pre-assigned seating and a first class section. What a difference this made. I purchased my ticket in a separate line, without waiting. I boarded the plane first and stretched out in a nice big seat. Adding to my contentment was the knowledge that this Aloha Air flight cost me less than I had paid for the other unpleasant experience.

On another occasion, my associate Tom and I needed to travel to Denver for a business presentation. Tom booked a room in a Courtyard by Marriott, while I did a little extra planning on my own and found out that a nicer, full-service Hilton Hotel was less money than what Tom was paying for his hotel. My hotel had a plush lobby, valet parking, 24-hour room service, and most important, a clean room where I experienced a restful night, awaking alert and ready for the day. Tom, on the other hand, experienced no such amenities, and the entire next day he complained about his inability to sleep the previous night due to the discomfort he had experienced at his hotel. I didn't have the heart to tell him that my room cost two dollars less per night than his!

This story brings up another important point, about which I will go into greater detail later in this book: If you are seeking luxury travel at a discount, doing your own research and bookings rather than using a travel agent is often your best bet.

Business Travel

When traveling for business or at the last moment, you will find that you will usually pay higher rates than if you had more advance time in which to arrange your travel plans. However, there is a positive aspect to this. Hopefully if you are traveling for business you will be reimbursed for your expense, which should soften the blow a little. In any case, when you do have to pay higher rates, you will also have the opportunity to reap the same rewards as you would if you were that company's most loyal patron. Simply by paying a higher rate, you will be considered the *crème de la crème* of travelers. The reason for this is that travel companies are forced to discount most of their rates to remain competitive. Therefore, when they do have the opportunity to charge higher rates, they treat those customers royally.

Whenever you are faced with paying a higher rate, be sure to always receive additional benefits. Many airlines will automatically upgrade any passengers who pay a full coach fare. Additionally, some airlines will offer bonus miles based on your higher fare. Likewise, many hotels will upgrade you to their best suite and provide you with their club floor amenities. Make sure that whenever you pay higher rates, you inquire into what extra amenities and services you will get in return.

When I traveled to Lake Tahoe for a conference, I booked my hotel late. By the time I made my reservations, all of the special discounted rooms set aside for the conference were sold out. Therefore, I ended up having to pay a little more than one hundred dollars extra for my room. When I asked the reservationist if paying the higher rate meant that I would get a nice suite, she said, "I'll see what I can do." I ended up with a beautiful suite overlooking one of the world's most gorgeous lakes. Moreover, when I checked in and asked the front desk representative if this high rate afforded me any special amenities, she arranged for a complimentary one-hour massage.

Be sure to make it known to whomever you're dealing with that you are paying a higher priced business rate and you would like to receive added services and benefits in return. Be polite and diplomatic, but assume that extra amenities are customary in such a situation. They are. This holds true whether you are at the gate speaking with a gate agent or checking into a hotel. Let them know that you are traveling for business and would appreciate any special perks they might extend. Travel companies will cater to business travelers as they do to loyal customers because of their tendency to pay premium prices and because of the high frequency of their travels.

Keep Your Standards High

Later in this book I will reveal an abundance of secrets to achieving luxury while paying the same as or slightly above what you would pay for low-frills travel companies. In the meantime, bear in mind that as a cost-conscious traveler in quest of luxury, it is imperative that you seek out quality, service-oriented travel companies instead of choosing a low-frills airline or a hotel chain whose priority is volume rather than service. This point is so important it is worth repeating. Although occasionally you will pay a modest premium for luxury, do yourself a favor and plan your travels exclusively with a high quality travel partner. In return for being selective, you will not only enjoy more pleasurable travels, but you will also have the opportunity to build loyal partnerships that will earn you even higher levels of luxury.

By building loyal partnerships with your quality travel partners you will become ever more knowledgeable about how to most advantageously cash in on your loyalty with each company. Learning the particular idiosyncrasies of your chosen travel partners will involve trial and error and a little patience, as well as the know-how you acquire from this book. Nonetheless, because your goal is to build a long-term, loyal partnership, rest assured that you will eventually understand the ins and outs of your travel partners better than some of their own employees. And by keeping your standards of quality high in selecting the companies with which you do business, you will be rewarded for your continued patronage with upgraded airline seats, luxurious accommodations, and a wealth of money-saving amenities for a reasonable and fair price.

Key Points

- ***Pay now or pay later.***
  Chasing big discounts can lead to big disappointments. Make sure you know what standard of quality a particular company offers in return for their low price.

- ***Consider the value of your time and peace of mind.***
  When choosing the travel companies with which you do business, keep your standards of quality high. An inadequate travel partner can rob you of valuable time, and poor service can make traveling more stressful than it needs to be.

- ***Pay a slight premium for luxury and you can reap priceless benefits.***
  In some cases, luxury might even cost you less. In any case, whether you have to pay a modest premium, the same price, or even less than the ordinary traveler for an extraordinary travel experience, you're worth it.

- ***Become a straight-A student of first class travel at discount prices.***
  Understand the intricacies of your travel partners' programs and leverage that knowledge to enhance your travel experience. With the knowledge you gain from this book, along with the knowledge you will gain from doing repeat business with your travel partners, you will be able to insure that all your travels are first class.

4

A Contrarian Strategy

Traveling Against the Grain

Recently while flying from Los Angeles to New York, I sat next to a man who was just returning from a two-week stay in Bali. His tales of luxury travel at discounted prices set my mind whirling with plans for my own trip, for he had just returned from a true Penny Pincher's dream. For only $30 a day, he had stayed at one of the finest five-star resorts in Bali. As if that was not amazing enough, he continued to tell me that this rate included his breakfast, dinner, airport transport, laundry, local calls, and a daily international newspaper. During one of the weeks of his two-week stay, he believed that he was the only guest at the hotel. Despite the lack of guests, the hotel maintained a full staff, including a twelve-piece gamelan orchestra of drums, gongs, flutes, and strings. Without a doubt, he felt that this was the best vacation bargain he had ever come across.

At the time of this writing, tumbling currencies and a weak economy have transformed the once exorbitantly priced Asian continent into a bargain for savvy travelers. More importantly, this story brings forth the second fundamental principle of this book, "The Contrarian Strategy." Simply put, a contrarian approach to luxury travel means that you travel *at the times that the particular destinations and travel companies need your business the most.*

The contrarian traveler uses the same type of strategy as a contrarian investor. A contrarian investment strategy involves buying stock in quality companies that have had relatively low stock value. The contrarian investor avoids buying stocks that are currently fashionable and concentrates on those stocks and companies that are currently out of favor, yet have a quality management team or other desirable characteristics.

Applying this contrarian strategy to travel is quite simple. If your hotel and airline are overbooked and turning away customers, your business will have a relatively low level of importance to that company at that time. But if the resort or airline is currently experiencing under-utilization of capacity, your business will be more valuable to them. Because they need your business, they are much more likely to offer you the finest in luxury travel and amenities at the lowest prices.

The first economic principle I learned in college was that of supply and demand. When demand is high, supply will be low, and consequently prices will be high. Conversely, when demand is low, supply will be high, and consequently prices will be low. Contrarian travelers get much more than lower prices, for when *a travel industry company has low demand and high supply, a higher level of preferential service will accompany your lower prices*. Therefore, when planning your low-cost, luxury travels remember that the *trend is not your friend*.

After hearing my airline companion's tale of Bali, I called Robert and Cindy, the occasional travelers whom we met earlier in the book. I knew that they were planning their second honeymoon and were considering Hawai'i, since neither of them had been there before. I told them the story about my seatmate (which got them pretty excited) and suggested that we look into Bali, since they were working with a tight budget and really wanted a nice romantic getaway. We applied the contrarian strategy, which stood up to the test. My first call was to the Ritz-Carlton, whose recently completed property offers panoramic views of the clear turquoise waters of the Indian Ocean. Embraced by pristine white beaches, this is a true luxury resort. Robert and Cindy were very pleased with the results of our rate search. The rates ranged from an ocean-view room at $118 per night to a suite at $345. And then there was my favorite choice, a 3,200 square-foot villa with its own private pool and private beach for only $3 more per night than a suite. Upon my suggestion, Robert and Cindy opted for the ocean view room at $118 per night. However, when they arrived at the resort and saw how empty the hotel was, they simply asked the front desk representative who was checking them in if she would upgrade them to the luxury villa. She did. I will go into greater detail about how to obtain hotel upgrades later in the book. In addition, Robert and Cindy were also able to obtain two business class seats for less than the price of two coach airline seats. I will explain how that happened in the airline chapter.

On a recent trip, I was reminded of the consequences of ignoring the contrarian strategy. My wife needed to attend a conference in Hawai'i, and I accompanied her on the trip. The conference was held at the luxurious Orchid Hotel at Mauna Lani on the Big Island of Hawai'i. During the conference the hotel was near, if not at, 100% occupancy. It had been some time since I had traveled to a hotel with such a high occupancy, and immediately I remembered why.

The first reminder came before I even arrived in Hawai'i. Prior to our trip, I had called the hotel directly to obtain a room upgrade, but I encountered one obstacle after another. I called the reservation center, an in-house specialist, and the acting general manager, all without success. It was only after calling the corporate office of the hotel's parent company that I was successful in obtaining a beautiful, ocean-front suite alongside a magnificent waterfall. Fortunately, I had reached an excellent representative who secured me the upgrade. I did, however, need to pay a slight premium above my original rate.

The second reminder was when we arrived. With so many guests and so much chaos, the staff at the hotel was generally ambivalent and even neglectful about extending the smallest courtesy. It was certainly not the consistent kind of quality customer service that I have learned to expect from a luxury resort. I noticed this as soon as I pulled up to the valet parking stand, where instead of the usual warm greeting, no one noticed me until I had pulled all of my own luggage from the trunk of my rental car. When the valet did finally greet me, it felt insincere and rushed. The front desk representative who checked us in was new and apparently a little overwhelmed by the high occupancy level. Consequently he took an excessively long time to check us in and was ineffective in providing information about the hotel. As the bellman escorted us to our room, I attempted to obtain an entrance card to the hotel club level (which offers enhanced amenities such as free food and beverage services throughout the day and a private concierge). Gaining access to the club level is something I am usually successful in accomplishing. However, my request was turned down, seemingly because the hotel was too full. Despite the beautiful room we had, staying in such an overcrowded hotel did not make for a very relaxing stay.

A neighboring hotel, the Four Seasons, seemed to have a similar ambivalent attitude towards quality service. My wife and I went there one day to tour the property with the sales manager and to have lunch. Although the rooms were very nice, the hotel was not willing to make many concessions in order to attract my business at that time; they were also close to full occupancy. Likewise, my wife and I were not impressed with our lunch or with the service. It took the waiter nearly forty-five minutes to bring us simple sandwiches. I can only surmise that this lackluster customer service was due to the high level of occupancy at each hotel and the scarcity of competing hotels in the immediate area. Of course, another explanation could be that I have gotten used to nothing less than the finest service, as you will, too.

PROFIT WHEN THEY ARE NOT

When an industry or company experiences financially challenging times, they offer incentives to increase their revenues. This is exactly what the airlines, hotels, car rental companies, and cruise line companies do to attract guests when they experience lower capacities.

The best time to travel anywhere is when everyone else is going to another destination. When a hotel is full to the brim with guests, as the above story illustrates, most often you will be treated like a commodity. That is because the employees will probably be too busy to offer you the kind of attentive service you should learn to expect. Conversely, when a hotel is only at 40% booking, the employees are going to treat the needs of each guest as a higher priority. This is the time when you will have the pool to yourself with a very attentive staff pampering you. The employees will have more time to devote to your needs, and they will increase their level of service to make up for the fact that there are fewer guests tipping them.

Increased advertising of special prices and media reports of industry hardships will inform you that a certain sector of the travel industry is not performing well. For example, a recent issue of *Condé Nast Traveler* offered information on thirty prime vacation destinations and the best time to travel to them. Hawai'i, which is usually a prized destination for many vacation travelers, was one of the areas covered in that article. At the time of this writing the Asian continent is experiencing an economic downturn, and because the tourist economy of Hawai'i is heavily tied to Asian tourism, the current Asian crisis has caused Hawai'i to suffer from a marked decline in tourism. As a result, normally high-priced ocean front suites in Hawaiian hotels are going for a fraction of their usual costs.

Remember that travel industry businesses will offer you their best deals and the most superior service during times of economic hardship or downturn. Thus, astute consumers can travel in an exceptionally luxurious manner while paying discounted rates and fares. So if you find yourself considering taking a trip to this year's most popular destination at the height of the busy season, think again, unless you are willing to accept average accommodations and service at an exorbitant price.

It seems that the news media and travel magazines spend an inordinate amount of time discussing the most popular travel destinations and in-spots for travelers at certain times of the year. Often, they illustrate the "Top Ten" destinations with colorful charts that indicate the great numbers of people heading to each particular destination. That's valuable information for you, because now you know where not to go.

UNDERSTAND BUSINESS CYCLES

Understanding how business cycles work will enable you to profit from downturns in the travel industry. Throughout history, all businesses have experienced good times and bad times. Any long-term business executive is accustomed to these natural and inevitable cycles, knowing that the cycles are usually predicated on the strength of the economy. What is important for you to understand is that although there will be times when the travel industry is strong, that strength will inevitably cycle into weakness, which ultimately creates a wealth of benefits for you.

For example, at the time of this writing, the airlines are experiencing an increased level in their capacity, resulting in profitability for the first time in years. Similarly, the American hotel industry is experiencing a high demand for their upscale rooms. As a result, airlines are adding new airplanes and seats to their inventory, and hotels are currently building new upscale rooms. This increase in supply and the inevitable changes in economic cycles will ultimately result in lower prices. An article in a recent issue of *Meetings & Conventions Magazine* stated that according to the accounting firm PriceWaterhouseCoopers by the end of 1999 there will be 517,000 luxury hotel rooms compared to roughly 487,900 rooms in 1997. In addition, Ritz-Carlton reports that they plan to expand from 34 hotel properties to a total of 50 to 60 in the next five to six years. They had 34 properties as of April 1998.

Eventually, this current good fortune for the travel industry will reverse course, and economic hardship will once again rear its ugly head. This is why you as a traveler want to take a long-term approach to your travel planning. Having a broad perspective and looking at regional opportunities is key to successfully traveling in luxury at a discount. You will see how to take advantage of current opportunities, and as the above examples demonstrate, future opportunities.

At the present time, the airlines are already faced with rising fuel costs, and full-service airlines are facing escalating competition and price pressure from the no-frills airlines. I have also been reading a variety of reports in newspapers and magazines that indicate some upscale luxury hotels are already discounting rooms due to a lack of demand, even in this booming economy. When these industries are once again faced with underutilization of their capacity, which should be even more drastic given the number of new planes and new hotel rooms being built, they will have no choice but to discount fares and rates. This will create plenty of opportunities for the penny-pinching luxury traveler. Therefore, your best approach is to be an informed traveler with a long-term approach to your travel planning. Stay on top of economic trends in the travel industry through travel magazines, news reports, and the Internet.

QUICK REVIEW

- Avoid the trends and the crowds, and reap the rewards of luxury travel.
- Understand business cycles; that knowledge will allow you to achieve luxury travel during times of economic downturn.
- Take a long-term approach to your travel planning. Today's economically strong travel industry will inevitably turn around, resulting in higher supply, lower demand, and future travel bargains.
- Read travel magazines, news reports, and research the Internet as part of your contrarian strategy. An informed traveler is a luxury traveler.

OFF-SEASON

You need not wait for an economic downturn to receive the lowest rates and the highest level of service. The discerning traveler knows how to take advantage of business cycles in all economic climates. And now, so will you.

Since I enjoy traveling so much, I like to be able to travel year round without worrying about the state of the economy. I also like saving money, avoiding crowds, and experiencing the most luxurious surroundings and the finest service. Consequently, I regularly travel during off-season times. Off-season travel is as beneficial as a recession. *Traveling off-season is one of the most fundamental principles you will need to keep in mind throughout this book.*

Off-season travel is a perfect way to utilize your contrarian strategy, regardless of economic cycles. Remember, if travel industry companies are busy enough to turn away business, they will have little incentive to offer you luxury travel at a discount. But during the times when they are experiencing underutilization of their capacity, they will be much more likely to go out of their way to get your business. This is especially true for upscale hotels that are expensive to operate and consequently have thin profit margins; they are happy to get any percentage of their rooms filled during the off-seasons.

Ed and Carol, the retired couple we met in the first chapter, have utilized the contrarian principle very successfully. As you will recall, Ed needs to travel in comfort due to his medical condition. However, Ed and Carol were determined not to let this become an obstacle to their enjoyment of traveling. Instead, they make it a habit to travel against the grain. They go to Europe in September, after the August holiday period, and when it's easier to secure first class seats and plush hotel rooms at discount prices. They take their cruises in early fall and late spring, when they are able to enjoy not only the good weather, but also the opportunity to book a luxury cabin for about 25% of the usual cost. They also stay aware of current economic conditions around the world.

Just recently Ed and Carol took a 21-day excursion through Asia and stayed in the nicest five-star hotels for less than $4,500. This budget included airfare, ground transportation, and lodging. Ed and Carol were able to achieve this amazing trip because during the planning stage I carefully researched hotels with them. First, we looked up various hotels on the Internet or called their 800-numbers. Then we inquired as to their upcoming slow periods. As it was, many of the Ritz-Carlton and Four Seasons properties were already offering exceptional deals because of the downturned economy. This contrarian style of travel has also resulted in lower airfares for Ed and Carol. On their trip to Asia, they flew first class from Phoenix, Arizona, to five cities in Asia and returned in first class for only $1,025 each round trip. Again this was achieved through carefully planning their travels. One technique that Ed and Carol used was to spend $200 on a one-year membership in their airline's private first class lounge. Since they usually travel at off-peak times, they are able to befriend the agents working in the lounge, which has been one means for their ticket to first class as well as a comfortable place for Ed to relax before flying. Like me, all of their flights are in first class, and they told me that their average ticket price is only $275.

In my own pursuit of low-cost, luxury travel, I have discovered several advantageous times of the year to travel to Hawai'i. Typically I will travel to Hawai'i in early November, just before the Thanksgiving weekend, or before Christmas break. I also travel in early spring, just before the spring break crowd, or in mid-summer. It has been my experience that at these times, the hotels in Hawai'i are not as busy. Consequently, I have been successful in confirming very low rates while getting the best upgraded rooms in the hotel. Remember that if a hotel can sell an oceanfront suite for top dollar, they will, and you will be stuck with an average room. And if you travel during a peak period, this will likely be the case.

When traveling off-season, you will also be able to obtain discounted car rental rates. I have often paid for a mid-size car rental during off-season, then was able to successfully upgrade to a luxury Cadillac DeVille because they were not in demand.

Bear in mind that following a contrarian strategy of traveling off-season and avoiding the in-spots does not mean you must settle for a vacation to Buffalo in the dead of winter. You can travel to beach resort locations during their so-called "shoulder" season or change of seasons. You can travel to Disney World while children are still in school. Your children might miss a few days of school, but with fewer crowds and lower rates, you will find that it is certainly worth the trouble.

Surprisingly, I have found that Thanksgiving week, which is usually considered to be a peak travel period, is an excellent time to travel to Europe. Because most Americans have a four-day weekend, you can travel to Europe without taking many vacation days from work. And since November is an off-season time in Europe, the crowds are thinner, which means you will receive preferential service, lower airfares, greater access to first class seats, and lower rates on upgraded hotel accommodations.

At times you will find it necessary to travel for business or for other last minute reasons and will not be able to avoid a peak travel time. When this happens, make every attempt to book yourself on flights that might have a lower load factor or at times of the day and days of the week when capacity might be lower. Consider flying on Tuesday, Wednesday, Thursday morning, late Friday night, Saturday, or early Sunday morning.

FOLLOW THE DOLLAR

When considering your overseas vacations from a contrarian point of view, also consider the relative strength of the dollar. The value of worldwide currencies can greatly influence the value you receive for your travel dollars. Because the U.S. economy is currently strong while competing economies are experiencing misfortune, the U.S. dollar goes a long way in other countries.

This is not always the case. Keep in mind that these cycles inevitably change. For example, during the economic cycle of the mid-'90s the U.S. dollar was weak in comparison to many world currencies. However, there was a notable exception, that being Italy. In Italy, the dollar and exchange rates were fairly strong. So instead of going to Japan in the mid-'90s, when you would have only gotten about 80 yen for 1 U.S. dollar, Italy would have been the prudent choice. A few years later into the cycle, the dollar regained its value, and the exchange rate had changed to approximately 130 yen to the dollar. Therefore, that would have been a much better time to travel to Japan.

Observing the relative strength of the dollar will enable you to make informed decisions when you plan your international travels; however, keep in mind that a weak dollar could result in a lower travel demand that in turn creates a travel opportunity. You will need to do your homework and compare the weakened dollar to the airfares and other rates.

Another way to benefit when the dollar is strong in the country you are visiting is to pay for your travel with the local currencies. You can do this for all of your travel needs, including airfares. One way to save on airfare is to purchase what is called a split ticket. That is, you pay for your outbound flight to a foreign country in U.S. dollars, and the return flight from a foreign country in that country's currency. Many of the larger travel agencies, including American Express Travel, can assist you with this. Following this strategy can result in monumental savings. For example, a study conducted by American Express, which compared the usual price of first class tickets with the split ticket price, yielded the following results:

ROUTE	REGULAR PRICE	PRICE USING SPLIT FARE	SAVINGS
Newark–Kuala Lumpur–JFK	$9,113	$6,260	31%
Chicago–Penang–Chicago	$6,167	$4,984	21%
JFK–New Delhi–JFK	$6,315	$4,984	26%
Cincinnati–Bangkok–JFK	$7,939	$7,371	7%

Note: examples are for actual first class itineraries, most of which involve multiple stops in different countries. The split price is based on the most favorable currency exchange.

According to *Condé Nast Traveler*, travelers can also benefit by paying for their hotel accommodations with local currency. At the plush Oriental Hotel Bangkok, one traveler paying in baht (the currency of Thailand) was able to secure a hotel rate equivalent to $180 a night. A bargain! For this rate, the traveler was not only privy to all the usual amenities of an ultra-luxurious hotel, but also to a chauffeur-driven, Mercedes limousine service 24 hours a day. And because it's the little things that can often add an extra special touch, when the hotel staff noticed that this guest drank Diet Coke, they delivered two six-packs to his room with compliments from the hotel.

Using foreign currency can also save you money on other aspects of your journey. One traveler quoted in the *Condé Nast*

Traveler article claimed that by using foreign currency for all of his travel expenses he was able to save over $2,000—enough money, he realized, for a return trip. My friend Lance told me how a devaluation in the Indonesian currency kept his costs down during a day-long shopping expedition. For the equivalent of only $4, he was driven around town in a clean, air-conditioned taxi for the entire day. His shopping was equally fruitful. He bought an antique artifact that would have cost him $308 before the currency devaluation for the equivalent of only $64.

QUICK REVIEW

- Off-season travel is key to luxury travel at a discount and allows you to use the contrarian strategy regardless of economic cycles.
- Off-season travel and avoiding the in-spots does not mean you have to settle for less than desirable destinations. You can still enjoy the most exciting places in the world, but during off-seasons you have a greater chance of doing it in a luxurious manner.
- The value of the dollar relative to other world currencies is an important consideration for the contrarian international traveler.
- When the dollar is strong, paying for your international travel with foreign currency can save you a lot of money.

TRAVELING DURING SPECIAL CIRCUMSTANCES

Another opportune time to travel is when a country has recently experienced internal strife. For example, at the time of writing Egypt offers excellent opportunities for cost-conscious luxury travelers. In November 1997, Islamic radicals massacred 58 visitors to the Temple of Hatshepsut, in Luxor. This tragic event resulted in a serious drop in tourism to Egypt. Now, many of the hotels that were accustomed to a full house and the ability to raise prices without any repercussions in occupancy have an abundance of empty rooms with a beautiful view of the Nile.

The decision to travel to a country that is experiencing or has experienced internal strife must be your own decision, which you should make only after carefully researching the current conditions. Having taken time to read various magazine articles and research web sites on the Internet, the information I have gathered makes me feel comfortable with traveling to Egypt. According to what I have read, major recent investments in the infrastructure have eased the way for travelers, and the Cairo airport has been upgraded and runs as efficiently as any major airport. Many hotels have been refurbished and currently have an abundance of luxurious rooms available. Most importantly, increased security is visible throughout the city and at all major tourist locations. The government of Egypt is fully aware of its economic reliance on tourism and has gone to great lengths to prevent further tragedies and to make tourists feel at ease.

You should carefully weigh the security risks of traveling with the desirability of your destination. For me, the improvements in Egyptian security and in its infrastructure are a vitally important consideration for traveling there. The lack of tourist crowds is also an enticement. Once-bustling sites where tour buses were lined up legions deep can now be yours to experience with relative ease and almost all to yourself. And finally, Egypt's incomparable beauties and the potential for luxurious travel also weigh heavily in its favor as a desirable destination. In *Condé Nast Traveler*, I read an account of one traveler's recent trip to Egypt. He stayed in Egypt's Old Cataract, the grandest of that country's famed hotels, where the czar of Russia and Winston Churchill once slept. The traveler had a room with its own fireplace, eighteen-foot ceilings, and twelve-foot-high French windows opening onto a terrace bordered by midwinter hollyhocks and fragrant basil and mint. The views from his terrace overlooked the Nile, passing *felucca*, and the desert landscape. For this traveler, the view was so enthralling that he started asking for wake up calls in order not to miss the dawns. And every night he sat transfixed as he watched the spectacular sunsets from his terrace.

This kind of luxury can be yours if you adopt a contrarian strategy. Following the crowd will reap inflated prices and a lack of quality accommodations or service. But if you travel when others are not, you will find that the level of service and luxuries you experience will be far superior to what you would find if you traveled to the most popular destination for that year.

Key Points

➢ ***Keep in mind the principle of supply and demand.***
When a travel industry company has low demand, they will have high supply. For you, this translates to excellent service and luxurious travel at discount prices.

➢ ***Travel off-season.***
Be flexible and travel when others are not. You will be rewarded with the best deals and the greatest luxury at the most desirable destinations.

- ➢ *Follow the dollar.*

  The relative strength of the dollar and your use of foreign currencies can provide you with substantial savings.

- ➢ *Understand business cycles.*

  The ever-changing economic conditions provide excellent opportunities for the informed traveler.

- ➢ *Remember the trend is not your friend.*

  To get the best rates, the most luxury, the highest level of service, and the fewest crowds, travel against the grain. Avoid the vogue or most popular destinations.

5

Airborne Luxury

Flying First Class at Coach Prices

Anyone who has experienced the incomparable pleasures of first class air travel knows that it's the only way to fly. And when you experience that level of luxury while paying only coach prices, your enjoyment will reach greater heights than ever before.

Although obtaining first class seats every time you fly may take some time, depending on how frequently you travel, there are many ways in which even the inexperienced traveler can obtain first class seats while building a solid, loyal relationship with one airline. Even if you fly as few as one to three times per year, by applying the principles and techniques outlined in this book you can begin to achieve your goal. My own experience proves it.

Since 1991 I have flown more than 500 times in first class, yet not once have I paid more than coach prices. In addition, I have had the penalties waived on refunding tickets, the restrictions waived as to when a free ticket or upgrade certificate could be used, and I have enjoyed the finest first class airport lounges throughout the world. I rarely wait in line to check my baggage and continuously receive congenial, attentive service from flight crews.

Even if you only fly a few times a year you will learn how to attain this level of service. How? By remembering this fundamental principle: Maintaining your loyalty to one airline. I enjoy all of these first class benefits due to my unwavering loyalty to one airline.

If you are an occasional, moderate, or frequent traveler, sticking to one airline only is key to receiving the maximum benefits. As I described in the chart at the end of Chapter One, occasional travelers fly three to five times per year, moderate travelers fly five to ten times per year, and frequent travelers fly ten or more times per year. However, if you are an infrequent traveler, which means you fly only one to two times per year, you will not have the same kind of leverage as the other categories of travelers. It will still serve you to fly as much as possible on the same airline and build a customer history that will ultimately reap rewards; however, if your goal is first class right now you may on occasion find it easier to obtain a first class upgrade on another airline. I will go into more detail on this point later in this chapter.

Although the next section has information geared to the infrequent or occasional traveler, moderate and frequent travelers will find valuable tips here, too.

How to Get First Class Seats at Coach Prices

You do not need to be a frequent traveler to reap enhanced benefits with your airline of choice. Even if you only fly as little as one to five times a year, there are many techniques you can use.

1. *Just ask*. One of the simplest but often overlooked secrets to flying first class at coach prices is simply to ask for the

upgrade. I was waiting to board a plane from Cincinnati to Los Angeles one day when I overhead a man, who seemed somewhat unsure of himself, ask the gate agent if he could be upgraded to first class. The gate agent said, "I'll have to put you on the waiting list."

A bit surprised at even this much of a positive response, the man said, "Oh no, that's okay, I probably wouldn't get it anyway."

"You never know," the agent said kindly. "Why don't you wait here during boarding and we'll see."

Shortly after I boarded the plane and started to enjoy my drink in first class, I saw that same man board the plane and head for the coach section. Towards the end of the boarding process, however, a flight attendant escorted him from the coach section to the seat next to me in first class. Apparently the gate agent had come on board and asked the flight attendant to upgrade this passenger. We introduced ourselves, and I asked him why he had evidently boarded the plane without waiting to see if he would be upgraded. The man, whose name was John, said, "My brother-in-law, who flies all the time, told me that the next time I fly, I should just ask to be upgraded to first class. I went along with it, but I didn't think they would upgrade me. After all, I usually fly less than four times a year."

I asked John about his travels and learned that this was the only airline he flew. I suggested that since he had accumulated enough miles over the years for future upgrade certificates, he should use those miles to always fly in first class rather than saving them up for free tickets.

I'll go into this point in more detail later.

During my first year with my chosen airline, I flew only three times. The second time I flew, I simply asked the gate agent if he would upgrade me, and he did! For the next few years with my chosen airline, I never flew more than 20,000 miles a year, yet I flew first class at least 50% of the time. In 1991, my fourth year with the same airline, I stopped flying coach. I flew first class every time except when I flew overseas. On overseas flights, I obtained a one-class upgrade to business class. Since 1994, I even fly first class overseas—every time.

The information in this book should considerably shorten the time it takes for you to reach the first class cabin. You may get your first upgrade on your fifth flight, your third flight, or even your first! All you have to do is ask. And once you've built up a mileage history with your airline, first class will always be yours for the asking.

2. *Look like a first class traveler.* The way you dress will have an effect on how travel companies treat you. If you dress in a professional manner, you will have a greater likelihood of being upgraded to first class. Airlines like to think of their first class cabin as a special area for VIP flyers. Therefore, if you approach a gate agent wearing a faded tank top and torn jeans, unless you are a major recording artist or movie star your chances of a free upgrade will be weaker than if you had a more professional appearance. By the way, this same approach holds true for hotels. If you arrive at a five-star hotel with a disheveled appearance, your chance of being upgraded to a more luxurious room will also lessen. Of course, a well-dressed look does not mean that you have to arrive in black tie or a formal gown. Dressing for success can range from a business suit to nice slacks and a polo shirt. The key is to take care in your appearance and to look like someone who deserves to be upgraded.

3. *If you have a full-fare coach ticket (which is the highest price ticket an airline charges for a coach seat), you can almost always be upgraded to first class at no charge.* Most people are not

aware of this. As I mentioned in Chapter Three, whenever you have a full fare ticket, be sure to ask for an upgrade. Many airlines will automatically upgrade full-fare ticket holders, no matter how frequently or infrequently they fly. Other airlines might require a nominal fee; however, if you are paying full fare, twenty additional dollars should not make a difference. Also ask to be admitted to the airline's private lounge. Incidentally, when you travel overseas on a full coach fare ticket, some airlines will not only upgrade you, they will also give you a free companion ticket, allowing you to bring a companion along without any additional charge. So whenever you pay a full coach fare, invest a bit of time and seek out the extra benefits.

4. *Communicate your present and future loyalty to airline agents.* When I initially started to fly, I was an occasional traveler who flew fewer than five trips a year, yet I maintained loyalty to one airline. Before I had accumulated many miles in my airline's frequent flyer account, I would do the following whenever I needed a special request honored, such as waiving restrictions or opening up a seat for me to use a free first class upgrade certificate: while talking with a reservation agent, ticket agent, or gate agent, I would say, "Perhaps I am not your most frequent flyer, but since 1987, your airline is the only airline I fly and continue to fly. In the past, I have always received excellent service from your airline, and I am sure that this will not be an exception."

By making such a statement, you are stressing your commitment of future loyalty to that airline—as long as you are satisfied. The possibility of your future business is the key for infrequent travelers, because it gives you leverage. Remember, even the nominal business you bring to this airline adds up over the years, especially when combined with all the other occasional and infrequent travelers. That is why the airlines still need to count on even the small amount of business you bring them in order to operate successfully. Besides, they know that someday you might travel more frequently, and if you do, they'd rather you travel on their airline. Whenever I expressed my commitment to future loyalty, most of the agents saw this as an opportunity to keep me as a customer and were happy to upgrade me. However, I would on occasion encounter an airline employee who was unreceptive. In those cases, I remained undeterred and simply approached another airline representative. Without much effort, I would eventually find one who would provide me access to the prized enhanced benefits I was seeking, even with only a brief history of loyalty.

Keep in mind that this technique will only work if you're sincere about building a history with an airline. Due to the airline's ability to track and document conversations with customers on computer, if you habitually try to disingenuously obtain upgrades, get restrictions waived, or do not really try to build a history with an airline, the airline will spot the pattern in your computerized customer history and end up denying your requests. Honesty is key. Do say that you have flown their airline in the past, are flying on it now, and intend to continue flying on it in the future—as long as you continue to receive the good service you have come to know.

When communicating your honest intent to be a loyal customer, you must also realistically consider the relative strength of your bargaining position. When you are just starting a history with your chosen airline and are a new customer, do not march up to an airline representative, claim to be the airline's best customer, and demand a first class seat. Do be vocal about your past, present, and intended future loyalty—but do it respectfully.

5. *Fly first class as much as possible.* This may sound like a catch-22, but it's not. When you are first starting a flight history with your chosen airline, it's important that you fly first class as much as possible. This will familiarize you with the ways of first class travel, and you will get a feel for how your airline deals with handing out first class seats. This will also help you when you're vying for a first class seat on a crowded flight, because then you can say to the gate agent, "Look at my flight history. I never fly coach—it's just too uncomfortable. Could you help me out by getting me a first class seat on this flight?" This really works to your advantage.

Believe it or not, very few first class seats are sold at a first class rate. One very important way for beginners to fly first class at coach prices is to obtain and use first class upgrade certificates.

How do you get these upgrade certificates? There are several ways. You can redeem miles in your frequent flyer account for free upgrade certificates. This is where the true value of ancillary miles lies, especially for beginners. Transfer as many points or miles as you can from ancillary programs such as your credit card mileage programs into the frequent flyer program of your chosen airline.

If you don't have enough points or miles for free upgrades, there is another way to fly first class at a discount. For a nominal fee, many airlines offer books of upgrade certificates or upgrades for individual flights. Often these books of certificates will cost as little as $125 for five upgrade certificates. Each certificate allows the user to upgrade one flight to first class. Some airlines, such as Alaska and Delta, allow passengers to upgrade to first class for as little as $40 above the price of the coach ticket. This is an excellent way to upgrade for a low price, and usually these upgrades can be confirmed before departure. (Please see the "Quick References" section at the back of this book for more information.)

If you are redeeming the minimum number of miles required by your airline for an upgrade certificate, ask the airline if there are any restrictions associated with this upgrade. You may be told that there are indeed restrictions, such as blackout dates or a limited number of available first class seats. If this is the case, ask your airline if you can trade in a larger number of miles for the upgrade in order to waive any restrictions.

When I first started flying with my chosen airline, I redeemed miles for upgrades and at times paid the fee for upgrades. This allowed me to learn the inside secrets of my airline while continuing to earn miles in my frequent flyer account. And now all of my flights are upgraded free of charge. As I will explain in more detail later in this chapter, the more miles you accumulate in your frequent flyer account from actual flights taken, the more rewards you will reap from your airline in the form of free upgrades and other preferential treatment.

Another way to get upgrade certificates is to ask your friends, family, and associates if they have upgrade certificates that they will not be able to use before the expiration date. Most of the free certificates I receive expire in a year, but they can also be transferred to another person if I'm unable to use them before the expiration date. I give most of my extra certificates to friends and family. One more thing: Never buy or sell an upgrade certificate—this is against the rules, and you could lose all your frequent flyer benefits with your airline.

After I spent some time talking with Carl, the frequent business traveler we met in Chapter One, he began booking all of his flights in first class. He uses the free upgrade certificates he earns from buying coach tickets and building mileage in his frequent flyer account. He also earns mileage points from his credit card, which he also redeems for upgrades. Because he always manages to fly in first class, he is always able to upgrade his wife Mary as well, despite the fact that she is only an infrequent traveler. When making a reservation for Mary, Carl will use his miles to upgrade Mary. If he has trouble getting seats for both him and his wife in first class, he will first get himself upgraded using his loyalty and established pattern of always flying first class, and then have Mary put on the waiting list, using his priority position. Then Carl calls back and inquires to see if Mary has cleared the wait-list. If she has not, he tells the agent that he is in first class, that he and his wife always fly first class, and that they would sure like to do so on this flight. Carl has told me that this technique has never failed him.

Here's an important note about using upgrade certificates: Try to confirm your upgrade before you arrive at the airport. When you book your ticket, make a reservation for the lowest available fare. Ask if there are any upgrade restrictions associated with this fare. If there aren't, confirm your coach ticket in first class, using your upgrade certificate. If the fare you've booked is restricted in terms of upgrades, ask for the lowest available unrestricted fare. I believe you'll find that the slightly higher cost is worth it to keep your first class history going, and for more reasons than that.

On a recent trip, I had the option to pay $267 for the lowest restricted/nonrefundable fare, as opposed to $307 for an unrestricted/refundable fare. I chose to pay the extra $40 and flew first class. This is in keeping with the philosophy I talked about in Chapter Three—it's worth it to occasionally pay a modest premium for big rewards. Besides, in a case like this, paying a restricted fare might save you $40 up front, but what would happen if you had to change your plans? If you have a brief history with your chosen airline and have not yet earned the privilege of having restrictions waived, you might end up paying as much as $100 to change your ticket.

6. *Seek out alternative sources for upgrades.* My friend Stella, who is an infrequent traveler, had obtained a new credit card that offered upgrade certificates on a certain airline. In the past, Stella, who flies home to visit her parents about twice a year, would usually seek out the lowest fare on any airline and always settle for coach. However, with this new credit card she thought that she would try to use one of her upgrade certificates and fly first class for a change. But on her first attempt to use the certificate, she had difficulty securing a seat in first class. So Stella cleverly called her credit card company and requested their assistance in obtaining the upgraded seat with the certificate. The credit card representative interceded on Stella's behalf, called the airline for her, and successfully secured the upgraded airline seat.

Because of fierce competition between credit card companies, these companies are often more than happy to assist their loyal customers to maintain a level of goodwill. As for the airline, it wished to avoid compromising its own relationship with its mileage partner, and therefore complied with the credit card company's request for the upgraded seat. Now Stella still travels home on a discounted ticket, but in first class. And she books almost all of her flights on the one airline whose mileage partner is her credit card company, which gives the airline even more incentive to comply with their now loyal customer's requests for upgrades.

Incidentally, this technique of cashing in on your loyalty

with one company to build an advantageous relationship with another works successfully with all partner programs, including hotel and car rental companies.

Richard and Kathy, the infrequent travelers we met in Chapter One, have also been very successful in using upgrade certificates earned from other programs when they take their yearly ten-day Caribbean cruise. Before Richard and Kathy took control of their travel planning, they relied on a travel agent who never quite delivered the goods. After I explored some options with them, however, they realized that if they used a particular credit card during the year they would earn enough miles for upgrade certificates on one particular airline. In addition, they have been able to obtain free cruise upgrades through their Auto Club membership. And now that Richard and Kathy are building a loyal customer history with one airline, they have the leverage to secure the first class upgrade seats when they need them. This works the same way with the cruise line, since they use the same cruise company each year.

The technique used by Richard, Kathy, and Stella is an excellent way to obtain luxury travel if you are not a frequent flyer. The simple strategy is to accumulate ancillary miles, which are miles not actually flown but earned from various mileage programs available through such sources as credit cards, long distance telephone companies, and even in some cases through paying your mortgage. Then redeem those miles or points for free upgrade certificates. However, if you are an infrequent traveler, make sure that the miles or points you earn are not restricted to only one airline. Many Visa, Mastercard, and American Express mileage programs allow you to redeem your points in a number of different airlines, as well as various hotels and car rental companies.

In most instances you will want to stick with the same airline by buying discounted coach tickets and using your points or miles to upgrade to first class. However, during some peak periods you might find it difficult to obtain the first class award seats on your chosen airline, because each flight only allocates a certain number of seats for free tickets or free upgrades. And if you are an infrequent traveler like Richard and Kathy or Stella, you might not have enough of a customer history to persuade the airline to open up another seat for you. Therefore, infrequent travelers need to have the flexibility to shop around with other airlines for their availability of award seats.

Likewise, there will be occasions when one airline might be offering a special deal for their upgrade certificates, in which they require fewer miles than your chosen airline does for an upgrade. In these cases, as an infrequent traveler you would want to have the flexibility to take advantage of those opportunities. To shop around for the best deals on upgrade certificates, do your research on the Internet or in *InsideFlyer Magazine*. Although you will not be building a strong history with one airline, you can still cash in on your loyal relationship with another company, such as a credit card company.

When occasional travelers are looking for upgrade opportunities, it pays to be resourceful and research all options. Robert and Cindy, the occasional travelers we met in Chapter One, not only found a way to upgrade their flight from coach when they took their romantic trip to Bali, but also ended up saving money in the process. When they first began to make their plans, they were offered coach tickets through a travel agent for a total of $1,690, or $845 each. That would have left them with only $810 in their travel budget. After asking the travel agent to find them a better deal, the agent came back with the opportunity to buy a business class ticket and get a free companion ticket by using a certain credit card. At the time,

Robert and Cindy did not have this credit card, but they called the credit card company and were able to get a quick approval. Unfortunately, in order to qualify for the free companion ticket, the card holder had to have purchased a certain dollar amount on the card within a certain period of time. Robert and Cindy had enough incentive to ask that this requirement be waived, and the credit card company complied. As a result, these occasional travelers on a tight budget were able to obtain two business class seats for a total of $1,200. What Robert and Cindy learned here was that many companies can be flexible if you only ask. You, too, should look for legitimate upgrade opportunities, and don't discount those opportunities because you think you might not qualify. Incidentally, when they were about to board their flight to Bali, Robert and Cindy were upgraded from business class to first, because Robert casually told a gate agent that this was their first real vacation in years and was also a second honeymoon.

If you are an occasional or infrequent traveler, you will probably not find free first class upgrades for all of your travels. Because award seats are in limited supply for the less frequent traveler, it is wise to book your travel as far in advance as possible to increase your chances.

QUICK REVIEW

- Don't hesitate to ask for an upgrade, even if you are a first time passenger on the airline and do not have an upgrade certificate. You may just get that first class seat.
- Look like a first class traveler. If you dress the part, you'll be more likely to get the upgrade.
- If you have a full coach fare ticket, make sure you get

upgraded to first class. This is almost always automatically available at no extra charge.

- When seeking first class upgrades or making any special requests, communicate your present and intended future loyalty to airline agents. The possibility of your future business is what gives occasional and infrequent travelers leverage.
- Fly first class as much as possible, using upgrade certificates. Exchange your frequent flyer miles for upgrade certificates, pay the nominal fee if necessary, and ask your friends and family to give you certificates they cannot use.
- If you haven't accumulated enough miles with your airline to get free upgrades, seek out alternative sources for upgrade opportunities, such as credit cards and long distance companies.

If you are just starting your history with your chosen airline, don't stop reading here—there are many more valuable tips for you in the rest of this chapter, too!

Flying First Class at Coach Prices

INFORMATION AND TECHNIQUES FOR ALL LEVELS OF TRAVELERS

THE TRUTH ABOUT FREQUENT FLYER MILES

There are many myths and misconceptions about the value of frequent flyer program miles. And there are secrets to getting the most out of your miles.

What most people don't realize is that the widespread availability of air miles has diminished their value. As I mentioned earlier, today's consumer earns miles through a myriad of methods, from credit cards to car rentals to dining out. This profusion of miles has created a situation in which there are too many miles chasing too few awards.

The vast numbers of consumers attempting to exchange miles for tickets has prompted the airlines to restrict the number of award seats available, and with good reason. A Wall Street analyst recently said that if all the air miles held by consumers were cashed in at once, a year's worth of revenue would be wiped out. As a result, award-seeking travelers are required to confirm travel plans far in advance, often as much as one year. And if they need to change their plans, they often risk losing their confirmed seats.

Consequently, knowledgeable travelers forgo complex and burdensome methods of exchanging their air miles for tickets. Instead, they purchase easily obtainable discounted airline tickets on their one airline of choice. Then, they use their powerful positions as loyal customers to get upgraded to first class and waive any restrictions. And not only do they accumulate additional miles, they accumulate the kind of miles that reap first class rewards.

The kind of miles I'm talking about are *base* miles. Base miles are the miles you've actually flown, not the miles you've accumulated from a broad spectrum of secondary sources.

IT'S NOT SIMPLY HOW MANY MILES YOU HAVE THAT COUNTS, IT'S WHAT KIND.

The airlines reward those travelers who provide them with income. Therefore, airlines do not look at your total point accumulation when assessing whether or not they will make special accommodations for you. They only consider your base miles.

This is great news for new or infrequent travelers. If you have only flown twice on your chosen airline, you have more bargaining power to get preferential treatment than a person who has never flown that airline but has 200,000 miles earned from ancillary programs.

I don't mean to say that accumulating miles from secondary sources has no value. It does. You can redeem those miles for first class upgrade certificates for you, your family, and your friends. This strategy is particularly useful for those of you who are first starting out your flight history with your chosen airline and have not yet accumulated enough base miles to earn automatic upgrades. After you have accumulated base mileage on your chosen airline, make sure you use those miles wisely. It is a big waste to exchange your base miles for free tickets every time you accumulate enough. Instead, you should exchange your base miles for first class upgrade certificates and your secondary miles for upgrade certificates and free tickets for friends and family members. And continue building your own base miles.

Remember, base miles are the miles that are earned from actually flying, excluding bonus miles. Therefore, purchase discounted tickets, earn more base miles, get upgraded to first class, and establish a strong history of loyalty with your airline.

The important thing to remember is this: *Your new mission is not to build the most miles, but to build the most base miles with the same airline to reach the highest level of loyalty possible. It is this kind of loyalty that the airlines reward with first class seats.*

Using powerful computer databases, airlines track every aspect of their passengers' histories and separately account for base miles versus all other sources of miles. This information tells a gate agent whom they should upgrade to first class when the coach section is full, to whom they should assign a priority position on a wait list, and for whom they will waive restrictions and penalties. And if your frequent flyer account contains only base miles, and you trade in some of those miles for a free first class upgrade, you will not diminish your leverage. The airline will still retain a record of how many base miles you've earned that year, and throughout your history with the airline.

Now that we've established the value of accumulating as many base miles as possible with the same airline, your first step will be to choose the one airline with which you will build your loyalty. Establishing a loyal relationship is imperative for all but the most infrequent travelers. Any history of actual flight activity will outweigh all the ancillary miles transferred into your frequent flyer account. No matter what, do not deviate from your carrier of choice. Remember, this will be a fruitful, long-term relationship yielding first class travel well into the future.

HOW TO CHOOSE AN AIRLINE

My friend Bob needed to fly to Tucson for a business trip and made a reservation on a Southwest Airlines flight. Forty-five minutes prior to take off, Bob arrived at the airport. First, he had to wait in a long line to check his baggage. Then, after waiting for what felt like hours at the gate to secure a seat, Bob actually missed his flight. His luggage, however, arrived in Tucson without him. To add to his misery, he was unable to get a new flight until the next day and missed an important business meeting.

If only poor Bob had done his travel homework, he would have known how to avoid such disappointments. He would have read up on the various major airlines and been familiar with their advantages and disadvantages, and he would have chosen the one airline that would meet most of his needs. As I mentioned in Chapter Two, if you choose Southwest, you may get a reservation, but you may not actually get on the plane. And if you do get on the plane, you are forced to scramble for a seat, as there is no pre-assigned seating. That means that arriving at the airport 45 minutes before a Southwest flight takes off will probably not be enough time.

Although most major carriers offer similar routes and almost identical fares, you will want to take the following into consideration when making your choice.

1. Find an airline that provides convenient scheduling from your home airport and best serves the routes you fly the most. Also consider with whom the airline has code share or alliance agreements.

As discussed in Chapter Two, these are reciprocal agreements in which two or more air carriers agree to accommodate each other's passengers. This benefits consumers because they can continue to purchase and book tickets with their chosen airline while flying on a code share or alliance airline, and still earn base miles on their chosen airline. This type of arrangement helps customers continue to build loyalty while allowing them flexibility in their travels. Be aware, however, that your airline may, from time to time, discontinue certain code share agreements and form new ones with other airlines. Therefore, be sure to read the information included with your frequent flyer statements to stay apprised of any changes.

2. Find out everything you can about the airline's frequent flyer program and its financial solidity.

You may be tempted to choose an airline that offers generous frequent flyer rewards; however, be sure to find out if this carrier is financially sound. If your chosen airline goes belly up, you'll end up starting from square one with a new airline. Do your research into an airline's financial solidity by reading publications such as *The Wall Street Journal*, *Condé Nast Traveler*, *InsideFlyer Magazine*, and by contacting the U.S. Department of Transportation. (www.dot.gov). It's generally safest to choose from a group of major carriers, such as Delta, American, Northwest, or United.

When you're investigating the relative benefits of various frequent flyer programs, it's important to understand the rules and restrictions imposed on using upgrade certificates. Find out how many miles you need to get upgrades and what type of fares qualify for upgrades. Again, this is where the value of secondary or ancillary miles comes into play. Remember, ancillary miles are best used for first class upgrades for yourself and your traveling companions. The only time you should exchange ancillary miles for free tickets is when they are for family and friends.

The "Quick References" section in the back of this book offers comparisons of the major airlines' frequent flyer programs. For the most up-to-date information, however, it's a good idea to check with the specific airline yourself.

3. If your past flight history spans multiple carriers, you'll still need to decide to fly, from now on, with only one airline.

Unless you are an infrequent traveler, the only possible exception to exclusively using one airline is if you fly every week and can establish an elite frequent flyer level with multiple airlines within a year. If you do not fit this description, you will be better served by exclusively flying one airline.

4. If you already have multiple frequent flyer accounts with multiple airlines, see which account holds the most base miles.

If the airline with which you have the most base miles will best meet your current and anticipated travel needs, then choose it as your airline travel partner.

In keeping with the contrarian travel strategy described in Chapter Four, consider choosing an airline that is experiencing lower load factors; that is, an airline that is flying fewer passengers.

Do, however, weigh this supply/demand opportunity against the risk of the airline becoming defunct because of any possible financial difficulties. By the way, airline load factors are available in *The Wall Street Journal* and from the U.S. Department of Transportation.

5. Flying exclusively with one air carrier is easier than you might think.

Your only requirement is flexibility. When flying with your chosen airline, there will undoubtedly be times when you will have to change planes while another airline offers a direct flight for fifty dollars less. If you're tempted to go with the other airline for just that one trip, remind yourself of how satisfying it will be to sit in first class and receive preferential service. And in the long run, a small difference in price today will be a lower fare tomorrow. Your loyalty will pay off with preferential service and first class seats while paying coach prices.

6. What do you do if your employer wants you to fly on another airline?

Sometimes my own travel expenses are paid by another company. If the company gives me an airline ticket on a carrier that is not my chosen airline, I always re-ticket with my designated carrier. Sometimes it costs me a few dollars and a bit of inconvenience; other times it is effortless. But regardless, I maintain my loyalty to my chosen airline and enjoy the amenities of first class travel. This far outweighs any inconvenience. If you find yourself in this situation, speak with the person in your company who is responsible for arranging company travel. If they are unable to approve a change of airlines, try to get your manager's approval. Explain that you'd like to use your chosen airline, and stress that the airfare will not exceed what your company would normally pay. If your company insists on ticketing with their usual airline, exchange the ticket yourself for a ticket with your chosen airline. Most business travel tickets are refundable tickets. Make sure, of course, that this will not violate a company rule and invoke disciplinary action.

Most major carriers have very similar routes and fares. Therefore, there is no advantage to changing airlines. The advantages of consistently flying the same airline, however, are tremendous. The essential thing to remember is that by maintaining and building a history you will gain preferential service and bargaining power.

The following are the results of a study I conducted of my own travel spending. I wanted to see how much extra money I was spending on airline tickets by sticking faithfully to my chosen airline. By tracking 150 flights to various cities, I compared what I paid for flying my chosen airline with the lowest available fare on another airline. *Guess what?* Although some individual flights cost me more, sticking to one airline for all 150 flights actually saved me money.

Cost for 150 flights on my chosen airline	$63,080.80
Lowest available fares on other airlines	$64,680.88
Cost difference/savings	$1,600.08

Based on a random sample of 150 flights, comparing my chosen airline to lowest available fare for the same routing.

QUICK REVIEW

- Base miles—the miles you earn by flying—give you far more leverage than ancillary miles when you wish to obtain first class upgrades and preferential service. Remember, the airlines offer the biggest rewards to those travelers who provide them with income.
- The best way to use your frequent flyer mileage is to exchange base miles for first class upgrade certificates and ancillary miles for upgrade certificates and free tickets for family members. Buy discounted coach tickets for yourself, get upgraded, and continue building your own base mileage with one airline.
- Carefully select one airline for all of your travels, so that you do not need to deviate from it. Base your decision on the airline's convenience of scheduling and routing, code share and alliance agreements, frequent flyer program, financial solidity, and passenger load factors.

ELITE FREQUENT FLYER STATUS

Set your sights on achieving at least the minimum "elite" frequent flyer status with your chosen airline. To further reward loyal patronage, the airlines have established elite levels of frequent flyer status. Elite frequent flyer status can be achieved by flying a minimum number of base miles over the course of a year. Miles earned from hotel stays, credit cards, or any other ancillary mileage program do not count toward achieving elite status.

Elite-level frequent flyers have the greatest leverage for obtaining first class travel at coach prices. This is because when you qualify as an elite-level frequent flyer, you have demonstrated your commitment to building a loyal relationship with your chosen airline. In return, your airline will offer you a bounty of benefits that will make you the envy of the flying public.

Whenever airline representatives access your record on computer, they will immediately see your elite status and unquestionably extend preferential treatment to you. To the elite-level frequent flyer, first class service is second nature. Elite-level passengers represent only 3% of the flying public. Therefore, you should go out of your way to qualify for elite status, even if it means taking an extra trip at the end of the year.

Once you qualify for an elite level, you receive elite benefits for the duration of that year and throughout the entire next year. And only one member of your family needs to be at the elite level for all family members to benefit. Although it is not imperative, if you are commencing a history with an airline try to qualify for the minimum elite level as soon as possible. The "Quick References" section at the back of this book lists the benefits and mileage requirements of the various elite programs offered by the airlines.

Qualifying for minimum elite status is easier than you might think. Most airlines have two to three levels of elite customer status, each requiring a minimum number of base miles. For example, on TWA you can qualify for the minimum elite level with only 20,000 base miles over the course of a year. On United, Delta, American, and Northwest, you qualify at only 25,000 base miles. However, American Airlines now has a little-known program in which you can attain their minimum "Gold" elite status by flying only 8,000 miles in a 90-day period, and their "Platinum" elite status by flying only 16,000 miles in a 90-day period. Just ask American to enroll you. And if American isn't your chosen airline, you can achieve elite status with American—and Continental, Northwest, Delta, and United will transfer your elite status to their program.

All the airlines offer minimum mileage of at least 500 base miles per flight. So even if you fly short distances or take a quick connecting flight, you will earn at least 500 base miles towards your goal of elite level.

My wife Nancy qualified for minimum elite status with her chosen airline by taking only three flights in 1996 (from Orange County, California to Hawaii, Philadelphia, and Paris), at a total cost of only $1,830. And by the way, she paid only coach prices and used my upgrade certificates to fly first class on all three flights.

By taking two trips in one year between Los Angeles and New York or any transcontinental route, you will earn more than 11,000 base miles. Add in a few short trips, and you will qualify for the minimum elite status on TWA. When you fly overseas, you can earn between about 7,500 and 17,000 base miles, bringing you substantially closer to minimum elite status.

If you don't fly many miles per year, some airlines offer an alternative way for you to achieve elite status—by flying a certain number of flight segments in one year. (See the "Quick References" section at the back of this book for more details.) As a result, short flights that earn you only the minimum number of base miles will count towards your elite status. When I first started to build my history with my chosen airline, I mostly flew short connecting flights, which improved my chances of achieving elite levels. And I added to these short trips by frequently flying between Orange County, California and Los Angeles, California to pick up the extra flight segments I needed. This usually added about an hour to my trips each way, but this minor inconvenience eventually paid off big.

And occasionally my fare was actually lower as a result of adding on the extra flight segment.

Believe me, it pays to achieve elite status; you will be treated like royalty whenever you fly.

Elite status gives you more than just first class seats. Regardless of which elite level you reach, just by qualifying you will be privy to a wealth of benefits, including free domestic upgrades, which you can book at the last minute. Elite status also allows you to waive many restrictions, such as blackout dates on free tickets and change fees, even on discounted coach fares. And if a restriction still applies, your high level of loyalty as an elite-level passenger can give you greater leverage. You can push a bit harder for what you want, and cite your loyalty as valid grounds. Although your elite status is printed on the flight manifest, be sure to point out any elite status you might have when making your requests.

Most of the airlines offer special toll-free lines for their elite-level passengers as well as special lines at check-in, so you can avoid the long wait in the general check-in lines. Many of the airlines also allow elite travelers special access to their luxurious private lounges without charge, depending on the passenger's level of loyalty. And most airlines provide elite-level passengers with tier bonuses that can increase your base mileage and point totals automatically by 25–125% every time you fly. For most travelers, this means you can earn 20,000 base miles for flying only 10,000 miles. And you can trade these extra miles in for a few free tickets a year to give to family members and friends.

The higher your elite-level status is, the more benefits you will receive. On Delta, my chosen airline, I have achieved their highest elite status, Platinum Medallion. This status allows me unlimited first class upgrades that can be booked any time prior to flight departure, as well as free access to Delta's private first class lounges. I have flown first class from Los Angeles to New York for as low as $320 round trip, and from Orange County to Atlanta for only $237 round trip. I also flew first class from Los Angeles to Mexico City for only $265 round trip, and from Los Angeles to Europe for less than $1,000 round trip. It pays to achieve the highest elite level you can, but you will still reap tremendous benefits from even the minimum elite status.

Occasionally you might board a plane that has three classes of service: coach, business class, and first class. Most often these are international or cross-country domestic flights. Depending on the policies of your chosen airline, your elite frequent flyer status might allow you an automatic one-class upgrade from coach to business class rather than coach to first class when you book a flight that has three classes of service. Business class is more desirable that coach, but you will want to be in first class at all times. Here's how your elite status can enable you to get a first class seat on these particular flights. By the way, these techniques worked well for me when Delta had three classes of service on certain flights. Now, Delta has only two classes of service on all flights: coach and first class.

Whenever you arrive at the airport for a flight with three classes of service, ask the counter agent to upgrade you from business to first class. Usually this will be enough to accomplish your goal. When it is not, ask the counter agent to put you on the wait list for first class. Then go to your airline's private lounge and explain to the agent assigned to the lounge that you are wait-listed for first class and ask them to help you obtain the first class seat. This almost always works. If it doesn't work, proceed to the lead gate agent in charge of the flight and inquire into your wait-list status. This is an effective tactic, because the lead gate agent will look up your customer history on the computer and see what a loyal customer you are. Usually the lead gate agent will clear you at that time.

Each October, you should review your base mileage for the year to see where you stand in relation to achieving elite status. This will allow you to plan the next three months and seek out discounted airfares to achieve the prized elite levels. While I was writing this book, I found I didn't have as much time as I normally did to travel. When October came, I had 64,000 base miles with Delta. I needed 36,000 additional base miles to reach Delta's required 100,000 miles for their top elite level. I didn't want to give up my top-tier status, so I planned inexpensive trips that accumulated big miles in a short period of time. I watched the news for advertised specials and called the reservation agents at Delta to ask if they had special discount fares from either Orange County or Los Angeles. By keeping my eyes and ears open, I found one weekend fare offered at $156 from Los Angeles to Orlando. This allowed me not only to take my daughter on a long-desired trip to Disney World, but also to accumulate more than 5,000 miles. I also found a $535 fare to Paris, which netted more than 14,000 miles, and made my wife very happy. In addition, I obtained some bargain fares between Orange County and Atlanta, which gave me the opportunity to visit friends. All of the extra flights I took enabled me to obtain the additional 36,000 miles I needed, and the total cost to me was around $1,000. With the exception of the Paris flight, which was in business class, I flew first class.

Transferring Your Elite Status to Another Airline

If you find that you frequently have to fly another airline because of your company's travel or business policies, do not be afraid to inquire into transferring your elite status to the other airline.

Recently while waiting for a flight in Delta's private first class lounge, I overheard a conversation between two businessmen. One of the men said his company just changed his territory, and now he's flying routes that are more convenient with United Airlines. He had already reached an elite level with Delta and was very reluctant to give up his elite status. He called the corporate office of United and explained to their marketing department that he was an elite level frequent flyer with Delta. He offered to give his business to United if they would start him off with elite status in their frequent flyer program, and they agreed. He also talked about a United gate agent he befriended who was so eager to make flying United Airlines an enjoyable experience that he upgrades him every time he flies. And this situation is becoming more common. Continental Airlines recently announced that they would match any flyer's existing elite level with any competitive airline.

On one of my trips, Delta had a cancellation and re-ticketed me on an American Airlines flight. I went to the American ticket counter and told the ticket agent that this was my first time flying on American Airlines, since I have always flown Delta in the past. I also mentioned to the agent that I had achieved an elite level with Delta. Eager for the chance to court my loyalty to American, the ticket agent upgraded my entire routing to first class and gave me two complimentary passes to their first class lounge. When I checked into the lounge and the receptionist saw my Delta flight history, she went out of her way to be courteous. She told me how I could get a complimentary one-year membership in their lounge. Incidentally, when I asked Delta to credit my frequent flyer account for the base miles I would have received if the Delta flight had not been canceled, they were more than happy to honor my request.

Remember, it is advantageous to maintain your loyalty to one airline. Unless your business needs dictate using another carrier or it's a one-time occasion, I recommend you maintain your loyalty to your chosen airline and build a strong history with them. Do, however, use the competitive nature of the airline industry to your advantage. Let the airlines know that as a consumer you have a choice, and they will fight for your business.

Quick Review

- The airlines unquestionably give preferential treatment to elite level passengers. If you are just starting a history with your airline, you should go out of your way to qualify for at least the minimum elite status, even if it means taking an extra trip at the end of the year.
- Qualifying for minimum elite status is easier than you might think. You can qualify on several airlines with as little as 20,000–25,000 base miles (or even less in the case of American Airlines' current program), and accomplish this in as few as two to three flights. Some airlines also allow you to qualify based on the number of flight segments you fly rather than on the number of miles
- The higher your elite level status is, the more benefits you will receive. But even at the minimum elite level, you will

be privy to free domestic upgrades, restriction waivers, special toll-free reservation lines, fast check-in at the airport, access to the airline's private lounges, and tier mileage bonuses.

MEMBERSHIP IN PRIVATE FIRST CLASS LOUNGE

If you are not an elite level frequent flyer, consider buying a one-year membership in your airline's private first class lounge. This is an investment that will give you access to the airline's lounge agent, the person who is accustomed to giving members preferential treatment, including seating upgrades. The annual fee can range from approximately $100 to $300. And once you have established enough of a history with your airline, you will be given complimentary access to these lounges. In addition to affording you greater opportunities for first class upgrades, lounges provide a quiet, comfortable environment to relax and have a drink away from the bustle of the general boarding areas. Many lounges provide computer and modem hookups, computer printers, and faxes. And some of the international lounges even have shower rooms and massage services.

BEFRIENDING GATE AGENTS: AN ESSENTIAL STRATEGY FOR ALL TRAVELERS

Gate agents are the folks who check you in at the gate counter and who take your ticket as you board the plane. I cannot emphasize enough the importance of knowing gate agents. When you want to secure an upgrade, gate agents are omnipotent and wield supreme authority. A willing gate agent can upgrade you from the lowest priced coach ticket on a domestic or an international flight to a first class seat. One gate agent I befriended upgrades me two levels of service (from coach to business class to first class) on a flight I frequently fly. And on one occasion when my flight was canceled, she took me aside and rearranged my flight schedule herself, saving me the inconvenience of having to wait in line.

There have been times when I've been placed on a wait list for a first class seat on a crowded flight, and gate agents I've befriended have bypassed other passengers and placed me in first class. One smart traveler I know named Sam has developed a very strong relationship with one gate agent at his local airport. This gate agent upgrades Sam's entire routing before Sam even arrives at the airport. And whenever Sam flies with a family member, this gate agent automatically upgrades the family member as well.

The best way to receive preferential service while building a flight history is to make friends with the gate agents at your home airport. Introduce yourself to them. Tell them you're an enthusiastic customer of their airline. Tell them how you look forward to being a loyal flyer long into the future. Ask them if they will assist you in building a solid relationship with the airline. Then, the next time you are at the airport for any reason, even to pick someone up, seek them out and cordially greet them.

Gate agents have their own internal hierarchy. Try to establish your strongest relationships with the lead gate agents, for they have the most power and authority to decide to give you preferential treatment. The lead gate agents of most airlines usually wear a uniform or coat that is a different color than that worn by the agents of lower rank.

Take note of the names and working hours of the gate agents you meet. I have befriended many of the lead gate agents at my home airport and at the airports I frequent. I ask for their business cards, learn their names, and ask what hours they work. This way, when I require special assistance, I know who to ask for. Even if that individual is unavailable, I give whomever I'm talking to the impression that I'm familiar with their airport, experienced with their airline, and therefore a more valuable customer. This results in my being offered preferential service in the form of bumping me up on a wait list, upgrading me from coach to first class on international flights, or whatever else I might request.

It pays to be honest, direct, and respectful to gate agents when seeking a first class upgrade. On one occasion, while I was in the beginning stages of building my loyalty with my chosen airline, I was flying with my wife from Los Angeles to London on a coach ticket. In my attempt to get an upgrade to first class, I approached the lead gate agent. I politely introduced myself and said, "Hi, my wife and I are flying with you today. Your airline is the only airline I fly, and I was wondering if there's any possibility of being upgraded. I know that occasionally you will upgrade some of your frequent flyers if upgrades are available prior to departure." I then handed him my ticket, saying, "As you can see, this is a discount ticket, but if you can assist in any way, I would greatly appreciate it." I also asked for his card and expressed my willingness to write a complimentary letter to the airline about how well he did his job. (I'll go into more detail about the effectiveness of writing such letters later on in this chapter.)

On any given day, gate agents deal with numerous individuals, many attempting to mislead them. They've seen it all and heard it all, and if you're not completely up front and respectful of the agents' authority, they'll know it. I came right out and showed the agent that my ticket was a discount ticket, and I was not pushy or demanding. In any case, the gate agent will know exactly what fare you paid and the type or discount level of the fare. Gate agents respond best to those who are polite and forthright.

While passengers were checking in for that London flight, I left the gate agent to go about his work. Meanwhile, I patiently waited near his podium, remaining within his view at all times. As the London flight was boarding, I again politely inquired into the possibility of being upgraded. The gate agent then handed me first class boarding passes for me and my wife. And he upgraded our return flight as well.

When trying to get a gate agent to upgrade you, it has been my experience that the adage out of sight, out of mind holds true. I do not board the plane, hoping the agent will come back and upgrade me. This seldom happens, and John, the man I described earlier in this chapter, was actually quite lucky that the gate agent boarded the plane to upgrade him. If you stay within the agent's view, they are less likely to forget about you, and you are more likely to get the upgrade. Although it is important to remain within sight and to follow up on your request, do be aware that gate agents are busy and try not to disrupt their work. Passengers who needlessly consume a gate agent's time or behave rudely will usually be ignored. Gate agents will appreciate your courtesy and will reward your thoughtfulness with their assistance.

It is also very important to bear in mind that an airline does not like to make a public display when it upgrades passengers. This could create an unfavorable impression with passengers who do not receive an upgrade. However, when first class seats are available prior to departure, airlines will upgrade loyal passengers. The costs to the airline are negligible compared with the goodwill it elicits. So when you request upgrades and ultimately receive them, take care to behave discreetly and do not flaunt your success.

Understanding how airlines view passengers and play favorites is what allows a traveler to enjoy first class while paying coach prices.

GETTING OTHER AIRLINE EMPLOYEES TO UPGRADE YOU TO FIRST CLASS

Although gate agents are the most important people for you to know, other airline employees can also give you first class seats and preferential service. Essentially, you should negotiate with whomever it takes to accomplish your objective. This could be the reservation agent on the phone, the counter or ticket agent at the airport (the person who sells you your ticket and/or checks your baggage), the gate agent, and even—as a last resort—the flight attendants.

When I first started to fly and my customer history was not firmly established, I often relied on the flight attendants to upgrade me.

Keep in mind that this is a delicate procedure. Discretion and tact are essential. Like gate agents, flight attendants are busy during boarding and deny requests from rude or inconsiderate passengers. If you've already boarded the plane, you'll need to have a compelling and honest reason to ask for an upgrade. I have requested and received first class upgrades from flight attendants because of a bad back, traumatic event, and excessive traveling in a short period of time. This combined with your loyalty can be an effective formula for reaching the first class cabin. Your objective is to be resourceful yet honest. Give a compelling reason why you should be upgraded to first class, but do not make up reasons; that would be dishonest. Normally it is best to approach the highest-ranking flight attendant or the friendliest. Like gate agents, flight attendants do not want you to advertise your good fortune when they upgrade you. Although approaching flight attendants is the most difficult method of obtaining an upgrade, it is your last chance, so don't be afraid to ask for what you want.

WAIT LISTING FOR FIRST CLASS

If you have an upgrade certificate or a free award ticket and are told that seats are not available, ask to be placed on a wait list. Whenever you are placed on a wait list, you need to exhibit a considerable amount of persistence and flexibility.

Your foremost objective when you are on a wait list is to be cleared from the wait list and receive the benefit you are seeking. Keep checking on your status. Prior to your day of departure, call the airline and ask how it looks for clearing the wait list, especially if you are waiting to confirm a free ticket.

I have been very successful in getting reservation agents to clear my wait list status when I call back and ask for their assistance. If my flight is full and it doesn't look favorable for me to clear the wait list, often the reservationist can recommend an alternate flight or routing that can be confirmed in first class.

Often when I travel with a family member, they fly using one of my free award tickets or a free first class upgrade certificate. When I make the reservation, I am frequently told that there are no more free first class seats available in inventory. However, by calling back a few times, I finally get an agent who is willing to make a concession and open up seats for my family members. Airline agents have a wide variance in the rules they can override. Therefore it pays to call back and find the agents who are most receptive to your needs.

If you are persistent on the telephone, you will usually clear wait lists before you arrive at the airport. However, if you have not cleared prior to your arrival, arrive at the airport early and again talk to whomever can assist you. Try to get the ticket counter agent to clear your wait list status. If they are unable, make a second request in the private first class lounge. If you are still on a wait list, make sure you inform the lead gate agent and ask if he or she will clear you. With a little persistence, you will usually find that being on a wait list is not a hindrance.

Reservation agents, ticket agents, and gate agents can help you get into the first class cabin with or without an upgrade certificate in hand. When you check in at the ticket counter, be friendly and engage the ticket agent in light conversation. Ask the ticket agent, "How does the flight look today? Is it very full? How does the first class cabin look? Do you think it might be possible for me to be upgraded?" They may say yes; they may not. If they say they can't upgrade you, be sure to say, "Would you put me on a wait list for first class in case I get lucky?"

Once you're wait-listed for first class, introduce yourself to the next agent (either in the private lounge or at the gate). Be friendly and make small talk if they're not too busy. Say to the agent, "I'm on the wait list for first class. Could you tell me how it looks? Do you think you can clear me?" If they cannot, tell them that you will wait patiently to see if the situation changes. Make sure to stay within their view while you're waiting.

Rewarding Good Service

Writing a complimentary letter is an excellent way for you to show your appreciation for an airline employee's exemplary service—and reap first class rewards for yourself. When you are negotiating with a gate agent or any airline representative for any type of preferential treatment, let them know you would be happy to write an appreciative letter to the airline that says how pleasant they are and how well they do their job. This is a great way to motivate the employee to grant your requests. However, do not give the employee the impression that you will specifically write that they upgraded you; this is not what they want in their employee file.

Most airlines prohibit employees from accepting monetary compensation from passengers, so your letter substitutes for tipping. Whenever a customer writes about an airline employee, the letter is documented in the employee's personnel file. Many airlines base merit increases and promotions on comments received from customers.

I will usually ask the employee for the name of their immediate supervisor. That way I can send a copy of the letter to their supervisor as well as to the corporate personnel office. This ensures that the employee receives a copy of the letter. The next time I see that employee, I ask if they received a copy of the letter I sent. This leaves an indelible impression of my goodwill, which they readily reciprocate.

Lastly, keep in mind that letters work both ways. If you receive poor service from an employee, warn them that you will write a letter of complaint. If they fail to rectify the situation, make sure to follow through and write the letter.

QUICK REVIEW

- If you haven't achieved elite status, consider investing in a membership in your airline's private first class lounge. This will give you access to key airline representatives who are used to giving passengers preferential treatment.
- Befriend gate agents whenever possible, especially the lead gate agents, and ask them to assist you in building a solid relationship with your airline.

- Always be honest, respectful, and discreet when negotiating with gate agents. If you're not completely up front and respectful of the gate agent's authority, they'll know it—and deny your requests.
- When seeking an upgrade with a gate agent, be persistent, but do be polite and considerate of the fact that the gate agent is handling passengers other than yourself. And remember, stay within the agent's view. They'll be less likely to forget about you, and you'll be more likely to get the upgrade.
- When seeking preferential treatment, negotiate with whomever it takes to accomplish your objective—the phone reservation agent, the airport ticket counter agent, the gate agent, the private first class lounge agent, or the flight attendants.
- If you are wait-listed for an upgrade to first class (with or without an upgrade certificate) or for a seat on a flight using a free ticket, keep checking on your status until you clear the wait list.
- Offer to write a letter to the airline praising an employee's overall good service whenever you receive special treatment. This is an excellent way of motivating an employee to grant your requests.

ADOPTING A FLEXIBLE, CONTRARIAN TRAVEL STRATEGY WILL PAY OFF

Being flexible is another essential strategy in getting favored treatment from airlines and those prized first class seats.

You are much more likely to get a first class seat if you fly on less crowded routes and at off-peak times. One of the reasons I am able to fly first class every time is that I am flexible with my travel plans. Often I will take a flight that is earlier or later than I'd prefer, or I have a longer layover in a connecting city to avoid traveling through a busy hub city. Sometimes I am flexible as to what day I travel. But it is absolutely worth it to me, because my flexibility allows me to fly first class every time. This more than makes up for any scheduling inconvenience.

Taking the time to learn the most advantageous times and routes to travel will pay off. With only a minor investment of your time, you will learn the best times to travel in order to get those first class seats. Ask questions when you make your reservations. Being a student of your airline will provide the information as to the most advantageous times to travel.

I suggest that you obtain a current schedule book from your airline so that you will know in advance what routes you want to book. You can easily obtain a schedule book by calling your airline or asking for one at the ticket counter. Often you can also find these books on board the plane. You might want to replace your book every few months, when updated versions are generally available. Knowing your airline's schedule will also help you to maintain flexibility, especially on a busy commuter itinerary in which some flights might not offer first class service. Your schedule book will indicate what type of aircraft is used for each listed flight. Simply look up the particular aircraft in the schedule book, and you will be able to see the seating configuration, which will indicate whether or not there is a first class cabin. Remember, if you are flexible, you will pay coach prices and fly first class every time.

Avoid the crowds and reap the rewards. It is very important

to learn what days to fly, what hub cities to avoid flying through, and what times of day to fly. If you schedule your flights wisely, you will have easier access to first class seats and receive more favorable treatment from airline employees. On flights with fewer passengers, there will not be many million-milers and super elites using up all the allotted upgrades and first class seats.

Bear in mind also that airlines only set aside a few seats in first class for upgrade purposes. But as it gets closer to the time of departure and they see that they are not going to sell the remaining seats, they will open up more first class seats for upgrades. If you choose a flight with a low passenger load, you are more likely to get the upgrade. When making your reservation, ask how full the first class cabin is. If it's pretty full, ask the reservation agent to find you a similar flight that is less full. If that's not possible, ask to be wait-listed, and keep calling back to check on your status. Also check on your wait list status when you arrive at the airport. People often reserve seats in first class and cancel or don't show up.

Travel when business travelers are not. Most business travelers depart on Sunday evening and Monday, and return home Thursday afternoon and Friday. Remember, Tuesday, Wednesday, Thursday morning, late Friday night, Saturday, or early Sunday morning are the best times to fly. It is at these times that you will be more likely to get first class seats.

Try to avoid traveling through major hub cities and busy commuter routes. When you fly a heavily-traveled route, taking advantage of free tickets and upgrades becomes extremely difficult. For example, between New York and Atlanta, New York and Boston, New York and Washington, D.C. on Thursday and Friday afternoon, you will usually only fly first class if you paid for it or reserved it far in advance with an upgrade certificate. In other words, do not count on showing up at the airport on those days and expect to receive special treatment. However, if you travel between those cities on any other day or on a late-night flight, expect to be able to write your own ticket.

In Atlanta, which is my airline's hub city, there are so many elite-level travelers vying for preferential treatment that even though I am a "million-miler" with my airline, I run the risk of being treated like a number and given no special privileges. That's because in major hub cities, the gate agents are just too busy to make many concessions. Therefore, if I do need to travel through busy hub cities, I make sure to do it at off-peak times.

On a number of occasions I have received preferential service by traveling this way, because the agents are less busy and friendlier and more accommodating.

When you don't want to leave anything to chance, you can fly alternate routes to your destination; you will usually have an easier time getting seats with a free ticket or an upgrade certificate. For example, if flying on Delta, avoid their major hub city of Atlanta. Instead, pick up your connecting flight in Salt Lake City or Cincinnati. This is where your research and understanding of your preferred airline comes in handy. You might fly a few extra miles, but those miles will be added to your account and you will enjoy first class service.

After you've achieved an elite status with your airline, you might try flying on the more heavily-traveled tourist flights. Most of the major airlines have flights that are geared for larger tourist groups who fly in coach, such as people traveling from Los Angeles to Miami to board the cruise ships. Usually these flights are overbooked, and often coach passengers will arbitrarily be upgraded to first class. Airline personnel know these passengers might never fly their airline again. But when gate agents look up your passenger record and see your loyal status as an elite-level customer, they would rather give the available first class seats to you.

Avoid traveling through cities where you've had unsatisfactory airline experiences. Being flexible with your travel plans doesn't mean you have to be inconvenienced. In fact, being flexible can mean quite the contrary. In my own experience, I've found that flying through a particular city in the northwest is something I avoid whenever possible. The reason is that I was unable to obtain a free upgrade for an overseas trip from both a private lounge representative and a gate agent at that airport. Here's where getting to know your gate agents works both ways. You'll find out which ones are accommodating, and which ones are not.

On that particular overseas trip, I ended up paying a nominal fee to upgrade my ticket. But as I emphasized in Chapter Two, it's occasionally necessary to spend a little extra to reap the rewards of luxury. As good fortune had it, however, the ten-hour flight allowed me to establish a rapport with the flight crew. When I arrived at my destination, two flight attendants spoke with the station manager, who upgraded my return flight to first class at no charge. The nominal fee I paid for the outbound flight turned into a free upgrade to first class for the return flight. And on my outbound route I met a business contact that should prove fruitful.

Your flexibility will also result in lower airfares. Many airlines offer discounted fares for a Saturday night stay. However, what they do not tell you is that you do not have to actually sleep in your destination city on Saturday night. When I need to travel for a Monday morning meeting, I depart on a late Saturday evening flight, arriving early Sunday morning. Not only does this give me a lower discounted Saturday night fare, it allows me to spend Saturday at home, and on Sunday I get to enjoy the city to which I've traveled. In addition, I save the cost of a hotel for Saturday night. Usually, if you call in advance, most hotels will allow you to check in early on Sunday morning. Most importantly, it is usually easier to get a first class seat when you travel overnight. Since many airlines use capacity controls on free tickets and certain upgrades, it is imperative that you maintain a level of flexibility in order to receive preferential treatment. Believe me, once you start traveling in this luxurious mode, you'll agree that it's worth it to be flexible.

Being flexible also means making use of your airline's code share agreements. If you make a reservation and are told that your airline's flight cannot accommodate you with an upgrade, ask the reservation agent if an upgrade can be made available on a code share flight. This usually works, although reservation agents seldom investigate this option unless you ask for it.

QUICK REVIEW

- You are much more likely to get a first class seat if you fly on less crowded routes, at off-peak times, and if you avoid stopovers in major hub cities.
- Take time to learn the most advantageous times and routes to travel, and to know what cities have the most accommodating gate agents. Be flexible and travel armed with this information, which will pay off with first class benefits.
- Avoid the business travel crowd, and you will be more likely to get an upgrade. Tuesday, Wednesday, Thursday morning, and Saturdays are best. Late Friday night can also be a good time to fly. And if you want to save money on hotels

as well as airfare, a Saturday night red-eye is a great time to travel for a Monday business meeting.

- If your airline does not have an upgrade seat available for you, ask the reservation agent to book you on a code share flight that does.

More First Class Tips

FLYING FIRST CLASS WITH YOUR FAMILY

When traveling with your family, it is a good idea to try to reserve as many seats in first class as possible. On some occasions you will only be able to reserve a few seats in first class prior to your flight. If you have at least one or two of your party already confirmed in first class, you can use this as leverage to secure additional seats in first class. You can tell an airline phone representative, counter agent, gate agent, or club room representative that you are traveling with your family and have already reserved a few seats in first class but would like the entire family to sit together. Usually these airline personnel will upgrade the rest of your family members.

Persistence and flexibility always pay off. If you are trying to confirm seats in first class and come across an airline representative who is less than helpful, simply end the call politely and call back. I was traveling through Atlanta recently with my wife, and we wanted to return home to Orange County, California on an earlier flight. The first airline representative we spoke to on the phone completely shut us out and insisted that there were absolutely no first class seats available on any flights that day. Undeterred, I hung up and called right back, and sure enough, the next representative confirmed first class seats for us on an earlier flight. This is one reason it's often better for the savvy traveler to make his or her own travel arrangements rather than go through a travel agent, which will be covered in more detail in a following chapter.

The earlier flight my wife and I took also flew a route that was different from the one we usually flew: from Atlanta to Salt Lake City to Orange County instead of through Dallas. However, this new flight was just as convenient as our previously booked flight and allowed us to return home earlier. This is also why it is important to be flexible. You are more likely to get those discounted first class seats.

HOW TO BENEFIT WHEN YOU'RE A DISSATISFIED CUSTOMER.

All travel partners make mistakes or have problems occasionally, and the airlines are no exception. When this happens, you can turn your misfortune into good fortune. The airlines place a high priority on customer satisfaction and service, especially for their loyal customers. And when something goes wrong, they are usually happy to make amends. When your airline makes a mistake, don't hesitate to express your displeasure.

Keep in mind, however, that you must walk a fine line. You don't want to be too aggressive or overbearing in your complaints, nor should you complain excessively. The airlines will document your complaints on computer, and those who complain regularly about petty difficulties will eventually be ignored. If your complaint is legitimate, however, do let your airline know that they did not live up to your expectations.

When you make a complaint, be diplomatic and assume that the airline representative cares as much as you do about the overall service of their airline. If you are treated rudely or unfairly, approach another airline representative and ask politely if something is wrong, since you have never before received such poor service from this airline. Also be sympathetic to the airline employees who may be just as much a victim of circumstance as you are. A polite and courteous attitude can really pay off.

On one trip from Fort Lauderdale to Los Angeles, storms in the Midwest caused a domino effect of flight delays and cancellations for my friend Laurie. She and a planeload of passengers were faced with the prospect of being stranded in Fort Lauderdale for the night. The airline was giving their stranded passengers hotel vouchers, but Laurie really needed to get back to Los Angeles that night. Laurie watched as the irate woman passenger ahead of her in the check-in line loudly berated a hapless ticket agent who could do nothing about the canceled flight. When it was her turn, Laurie smiled at the ticket agent and told him she was sorry to see that he had been so mistreated by the previous passenger. She also said that she really needed to get back to Los Angeles that night and was wondering if there were any way he could help her out. Appreciative of her polite request and her empathetic manner, this ticket agent handed Laurie a voucher for a cab to Miami Airport and exchanged her coach ticket for a business class ticket on another airline that would take her nonstop from Miami to Los Angeles that night. (Her flight out of Fort Lauderdale would have had a layover in a connecting city.)

When you have a complaint, be sure to speak to an airline representative who is willing and able to help you. If you are talking to a supervisor who is not accommodating or receptive, find a representative who will be more supportive. Fortunately, most airlines have a multitude of supervisors on hand. Do be extremely cautious, however, about making complaints to airline personnel while on board the plane. If a flight crew member perceives you as interfering with their work, you could be subject to a fine or worse. Chapter Eight will explore this point in greater detail.

When you voice a complaint, know in advance what you hope to accomplish. On a recent trip through Atlanta, I was on stand-by for a flight to Los Angeles, which happened to be one of the busiest flights between Los Angeles and Atlanta. When I put my name on the stand-by list 15 minutes prior to departure, I was at the bottom of the list. I approached the podium and politely asked a gate agent how it looked for me to get on the flight. He snapped at me rudely. I sought out a lead gate agent and explained my situation, firmly expressing my displeasure with the previous gate agent's behavior. I told the lead gate agent how often I encountered representatives of this airline and how atypical I thought the rude agent's response was. I said that I needed to get back to Los Angeles immediately, yet did not want to sit in coach, and I would appreciate it if he could get me on this flight. Not only was I able to get a seat on this very crowded flight, I sat in the very last available first class seat, which happened to be next to Bruce Springsteen.

If you voice your complaint and are still not satisfied, go to the next higher level. Ask for a supervisor, and if all else fails, call the CEO's office. Usually if you call the CEO's office, you will get an executive assistant. These people are very helpful; however, they do need to be treated delicately. If you call their office and behave aggressively, they will not be very accommodating. You need to approach them from a position of concern for the airline's reputation. After all, you are a loyal customer. And before you call an executive's office, make sure you have documented your prior attempts to have the problem resolved. Calling the CEO's office is a last resort tactic, so don't make a habit of it.

Chapter Eight will explore in greater detail effective techniques for expressing dissatisfaction to the airlines and your other travel partners, which can help you turn travel misfortunes into fortune.

In the meantime, give yourself the opportunity to start putting the knowledge and advice in this chapter to work for you. Experiment with the techniques, and you'll be surprised at how easy it will be to achieve your goals. You'll also be surprised at how easy it will be to get used to those first class seats.

Key Points

➢ ***Make the choice for first class by being a loyal customer to one airline.***

Unless you are an infrequent traveler, your unwavering loyalty to one airline is the most important key to flying first class every time. So choose your airline wisely and be rewarded for your steadfast loyalty.

➢ ***Reach your first class goal with minimal effort, even if you're just starting out.***

Ask for what you want, express your current and intended future loyalty, fly first class as often as possible using upgrade certificates, and take advantage of getting upgraded when you hold a full coach fare.

➢ ***Use your frequent flyer program wisely.***

Regardless of how many ancillary miles you earn, the airlines provide the greatest number of benefits to the passengers who provide them with income. That means you should concentrate on building base miles—those miles actually flown. Trade in your ancillary miles for free first class upgrades and for free tickets for your traveling companions. Trade your base miles in for free upgrades. Buy discounted tickets for yourself and continue building base miles to receive a vast array of benefits.

➢ ***Fly at the elite level; it is a worthwhile goal.***
When you achieve even the minimum elite frequent flyer level, you will be in an enviable position that wields the most leverage when seeking special treatment.

➢ ***Ask and you shall receive, when seeking upgrades or other special concessions.***
Although gate agents have the most power to upgrade you, be creative in enlisting the aid of anyone who can help you. Reservation agents, ticket agents, first class lounge agents, and even flight attendants can upgrade you and grant your requests.

➢ ***Write an appreciative letter to your airline, whenever you receive preferential treatment.***
This is a powerful motivation for airline employees to grant your special requests.

➢ ***Use the contrarian approach to achieve first class by traveling against the grain.***
You are more likely to get upgraded if you travel less-busy routes and at off-peak times.

6

Fit For a King

Sleeping at Five-Star Hotels at a Fraction of the Cost

My friend Lance, a moderate traveler who regularly travels to the Inter-Continental Hotel in Seoul, Korea, told me that whenever he checks in, he is escorted through a private entrance, followed by an entourage of the hotel's staff. He is pampered with a massage, and in his room is a complimentary bottle of champagne, a bottle of scotch, fruit, cheeses, and a plate of exquisite chocolates. After regaling me with all the details of this VIP treatment, he proved his astuteness as a consumer when he said, "And I get all this for less than the price of a cheap motel."

Once you arrive at your destination, having enjoyed incomparable comforts as a first class air passenger, there is no need to start compromising now by settling for a less than luxurious hotel room.

Picking the Right Hotel

There is an old adage that is resoundingly accurate when seeking luxurious hotel accommodations: *You get what you pay for.*

As you will recall from Chapter One, there is a tremendous difference between the level of service offered at a four- or five-star hotel and an average hotel. An upscale hotel will be an oasis away from the bustling streets. It will provide you with much-needed pampering after a long day of business meetings, sightseeing, or shopping. Having traveled throughout the world, I have spent the night in all sorts of hotel beds. And let me tell you, there is no substitute for a spacious, elegant, and quiet room with a spectacular view, and a comfortable bed with ultra-soft pillows and a fluffy down comforter. Most importantly, the hotel you choose will have a crucial impact on the satisfaction of your trip. A fine hotel will give your journey an overall feeling of luxury, because your hotel is the number one place to experience quiet indulgence and VIP treatment.

You need not be wealthy to enjoy the finest hotels in the world. However, as discussed in Chapter Three, you might need to pay a nominal premium for upscale hotels. Hotels will be the most common travel companies in which you might find it necessary to pay a bit more for quality. However, by following the advice in this chapter, most often you will be able to enjoy a first class hotel for the same price as an average hotel. But since the value of the luxurious experience you can have in an upscale hotel is immeasurable, any small premium you might have to pay is well worth the money.

Frequent Guest Programs

What makes it possible to enjoy a luxurious five-star hotel while paying only discounted prices? The simple answer is the competitive nature of the hotel industry. Like most other kinds of travel companies, the hotel industry is a highly competitive business that is vulnerable to certain economic cycles. To get through tough economic times and to build up a loyal customer base, the hotel industry designed frequent guest programs that are similar to the airlines' frequent flyer programs.

Most of the major hotel chains, including Hilton, Sheraton, Hyatt, Holiday Inn, Westin, and Marriott, offer frequent guest programs. And although some of the very upscale hoteliers such as the Ritz-Carlton do not actively promote a frequent guest program, they do track their guests' customer histories and make special accommodations and upgrades available to their most loyal guests.

Here is how customer loyalty can enable you to secure the best rooms in the most luxurious hotels at a discount price. One of my favorite vacation spots is Maui, Hawai'i. While in Hawai'i I stay at the Ritz-Carlton Kapalua. Whenever I travel to Kapalua it is during the off-season, which ensures that I pay the lowest price for a first class room. When I make my reservations, I reserve their lowest-priced room. Upon my arrival at the hotel, I tell the front desk representative how happy I am to be returning to their hotel. When the front desk representative checks the computer and sees that I have established a history as a frequent guest at this particular property, and at the Ritz-Carlton Hotels in general, he or she usually upgrades me to an ocean front suite with a price tag far in excess of the room I reserved, and usually at no additional cost.

Likewise, Lance's experience with luxury hotels is not limited to the Inter-Continental in Seoul. He also enjoys staying at many of the Four Seasons Hotels. Whenever he stays at a Four Seasons Hotel he always makes it a habit to introduce himself to the general manager of the property. He tells them how much he enjoys the quality of the Four Seasons and that he is happy to be able to stay at this property. Usually the manager offers Lance a complimentary upgrade, and sometimes drinks in the lounge or a complimentary dinner in the restaurant. Whenever Lance plans to stay at a Four Seasons Hotel where he has not been before, he calls upon one of those general managers, who readily assist him in getting a great rate at the property he plans to visit. Very often the manager will call the property manager at the other Four Seasons and request VIP treatment for Lance. This usually results in a nice room upgrade. Even though the Four Seasons Hotels do not have a frequent guest program per se, Lance has been very successful in cashing in on the loyalty he has established to enhance his future visits.

Like the airline frequent flyer programs, the hotel industry's frequent guest programs provide the average traveler entrée to a world of luxurious benefits. However, you will need to follow a strategy that is somewhat different from the strategy outlined for the airline frequent flyer programs. Rather than stick to one particular hotel chain, you should join a few select frequent guest programs and remain loyal to those few programs. The main reason for this is flexibility. Enrolling in the frequent guest programs of a select few hotels will provide you with the flexibility you need to insure first class hotel accommodations every time.

To explain, unlike the major competing air carriers who tend to offer similar services and rates, hotels are not always so consistent. When you fly on your chosen airline travel partner, there is only one choice you need to make, that being first class. But when it's time to select a hotel, you are faced with a multitude of options. These options vary from low-priced, low-service hotels to luxurious full-service resorts—with an array of choices in between. To add to the confusion, hotels offer a rate structure more challenging to understand than the airlines' rate structure.

Even within a single hotel chain, you often need to choose between a confusing assortment of various types of hotels. Making the wrong choice, as I did in Fort Lauderdale at the Sheraton Inn, can result in an unpleasant trip. It's not that the Sheraton is an undesirable chain; quite the contrary. It's that the Sheraton chain includes a luxury collection of hotels, a group of business-level hotels, and two low-end groups of hotels called the Four Points and the Sheraton Inns. I ended up at one of the low-end hotels in the chain.

Another thing to be aware of is that within one particular hotel chain, a certain individual hotel might not be company owned, but rather licensed to independent operators. Therefore, even if a hotel carries a flagship name like Hilton, that does not necessarily mean that the hotel is owned by the Hilton company. As a result, an independently operated hotel might not offer the same quality of service as the other hotels in the chain. Likewise, many older hotel properties are in need of renovations.

This "consistent inconsistency" among the hotel chains is the main reason I advocate restricting your business to the more upscale hoteliers, such as the Ritz-Carlton or Four Seasons. These hoteliers tend to be more consistent than other chains. Besides, these hotels will now be available to you for relatively the same amount of money you would spend elsewhere.

Another thing to keep in mind is that not every hotel chain offers properties in all locations. Unlike the airline industry, where most competitors offer similar rates and routes, the hotel industry differs widely, not only in terms of rates, but also in terms of geographical availability.

Therefore, in order to have the flexibility necessary to get first class accommodations and amenities at the lowest prices every time, maintain a strategy of sticking to a few high quality resorts and upscale first class hotels. This way, if the city you are visiting doesn't have a luxury hotel available through one of your chosen hotel partners, you'll have the option of finding a luxury hotel through your other chosen hotel partners. Do not, however, spread your business too thinly. Like the airlines, a relationship predicated on loyalty will reap you the greatest rewards.

It has been my personal experience that the Hyatt and Hilton hotels offer very good frequent guest programs. Both of these hotels offer tier-level frequent guest status that is comparable to the elite levels of the airlines. Based upon the number of nights stayed within a year, guests can achieve an elite-level membership. With an elite-level membership, guests are automatically upgraded and offered suites and concierge-level rooms without additional charge. Moreover, members of these frequent guest programs usually receive bonus points with each stay.

Many hotel frequent guest programs are aligned with airline frequent flyer programs, which gives you the option of transferring accumulated hotel points into airline frequent flyer programs. I have found it advantageous to convert hotel points into airline miles. Usually the reward levels with hotels are very high, and they seem to have a lot of blackout periods. By converting hotel points into air miles, I can earn more free upgrades and tickets, which allows me to bring more friends and family along on my trips. Usually there is not a charge for frequent guest programs, except for the Sheraton's Gold Program, which costs $25 a year. Even then, when I wrote to their program administrator, they waived my fee.

QUICK REVIEW

- Unlike most airlines, hotels vary in quality and service, even within the same hotel chain.
- In order to have the flexibility to obtain first class hotel rooms at a discount every time, join a few select hotel frequent guest programs and remain loyal to those programs.

CALL DIRECTLY, AND DON'T FORGET YOUR CONTRARIAN STRATEGY

While planning a trip to Puerto Rico, I initially encountered costly hotel rates through the Leading Hotels of the World's 800-number reservation service. I was told that the lowest rate for the location and time period I desired was $525 per night. As I was not satisfied with this rate, I called back a few minutes later and was quoted a rate of $350. This was still too high, so I followed one of my cardinal rules and directly called the front desk of the hotel I was interested in visiting. Just by simply calling the hotel directly, I was able to obtain an $825-per-night room for only $175 a night. That was quite a difference, and it was well worth the cost of a long-distance call to Puerto Rico.

The best way to maintain control of your travel arrangements and make that personal connection with a hotel is by calling directly. Here's why calling directly can make a difference to the penny-pinching luxury traveler. Calling directly accomplishes three important goals necessary to secure first class accommodations at discount prices: you can establish a relationship with the front desk staff; you can find out when the hotel will be at a low occupancy level; and you can directly inquire into discounts and upgrades. This third goal will be explored in the next section on rate flexibility. In my case, when I called the hotel in Puerto Rico directly, I was able to speak with the front desk representative on the actual hotel property, instead of dealing with a remote hotel reservation service. This enabled me to establish an all-important rapport with that front desk representative. Also, he was in a position to most accurately answer my inquiries as to which dates the hotel would have its lowest occupancy rate. Remember the contrarian strategy covered in Chapter Four? Booking at a time when the hotel would have a low occupancy was key in allowing me to confirm the lower rate and get the best room.

During our conversation I told the front desk representative how much I enjoyed being upgraded and how, when I am given preferential treatment, I reciprocate by being very generous. That was my way of telling him that I would generously tip him for upgraded accommodations. Do be aware, however, that you must be careful in how you approach a situation like this. As I will explore in greater detail in Chapter Eight, some employees do not understand the value of service, and you will be able to tell by talking to the employee. If an employee does not respond to your stated intention to be generous when treated well, do not push the issue. Instead, wait until you arrive at the hotel, then feel out the situation and perhaps ask the bellman to upgrade you. I will explore this option in more detail below. In this particular case, I was fortunate to be talking to a front desk representative who fully understood my subtle suggestion.

As a result of my direct call, I received much more than a low room rate. This particular front desk representative upgraded me to the best oceanfront suite in the hotel, tagged my reservation as a VIP guest, and showered my arrival with gift baskets. The hotel staff, who frequently deal with mega stars, treated me with great distinction and courtesy. The front desk representative also provided me with two complimentary golf passes for five days, a cost savings of $95 per person per day. In addition, he gave me daily breakfast coupons. In return for this treatment, I tipped him $100. At first glance this may seem excessive; however, considering the free golf and breakfast, I saved over $1,200, stayed in the best room in the hotel, and was treated like a VIP. I'd say that is a bargain for $100.

Because I called directly to establish a relationship with a hotel employee in order to get the best rate, I was able to spend a few nights at the most luxurious five-star resort in Puerto Rico for only $175 a night, a fraction of what the average traveler would pay. By making friends with a reservationist, front desk representative, or the bell staff, you should be able to achieve the ultimate in luxurious upgrades and VIP treatment at a fraction of the cost. And remember, your tips are worthwhile investments in low-cost, luxury travels.

Calling your travel companies directly usually enables you to negotiate the best deals. This is especially true when you call upscale hotels. Many upscale hotels are reluctant to advertise low rates, as they do not want to be grouped with lower quality hotels in the mind of the consumer. However, by asking questions on the phone, you will know when they are experiencing low occupancy. Most hotel representatives will have no problem answering your questions about what their occupancy level is and when to book in order to have the best chance for upgrades.

There is another very important benefit of calling directly, and this applies to calling hotels, car rental agencies, the airlines, and any other travel company. When you call directly, you have the ability to research your own travel plans rather than relying on travel agents, about whom I will go into more detail later. This personal contact and ability to make in-depth inquiries will provide you with the ultimate control and flexibility to find hidden travel treasures. On this occasion, with a brief phone call I was able to experience a luxurious trip at a fraction of the cost.

RATE FLEXIBILITY

The amazing flexibility in the rate structure within the hotel industry is a key reason to call directly. Moreover, this rate flexibility requires you to be persistent in exploring all available discounts when making hotel reservations. Keep in mind that there is a myriad of hotel rates to choose from, and that your objective is to get the best room at the lowest price. When speaking with a reservationist, attempt to ascertain what discounts are available for the specific property. Even though a hotel might be a member of a major chain, many individual hotel properties offer specific discounts for specific groups and organizations. By finding out in advance what discounts the hotel offers, travelers who are affiliated with those groups and organizations can cut through the higher rates and save time as well as money.

Often when attempting to secure reservations for a specific date and location, I have encountered numerous rate discrepancies. Last spring I found it necessary to travel to San Diego during a busy spring break week. All the hotels I inquired into were full except for the Sheraton. My initial call to the Sheraton resulted in a rate quote of $250 per night. This rate was the so-called "rack rate"; in other words, the rate the uninformed traveler might pay. Hotel rack rates are similar to the "maufacturer's suggested retail price" you might find while shopping for a television or other item. The important point for you to remember is that these hotel rack rates are almost always negotiable, especially if you follow the tips in this book. With this in mind, I made a few more calls to that Sheraton, and on my fourth call the reservationist informed me of a special Mastercard rate of $95 per night. And even though I did not have a Mastercard he secured the special rate for me.

Another thing to remember is that often when you check into a hotel, the front desk representative only has access to your rate and not what type of discount is associated with the rate. As a result, hotels seldom ask for corporate identification or any other membership cards associated with a discount. Remember that many hotels offer a broad range of corporate rates and special discounts, which can provide savvy travelers the opportunity to enjoy first class upscale hotels at discount prices. The following are just a few of the possible affiliations that can earn you hotel discounts: AAA, AARP, airline frequent flyer programs, credit cards, U.S. Embassy discount (especially when traveling overseas), professional affiliations, and corporate rates.

If you cannot obtain a free upgrade after securing the lowest priced room, find out what an upgrade to the next level of room will cost. Remember that with hotels, you get what you pay for. Most people are happy to obtain a low rate and to leave it at that, but you can also travel in style without being a spendthrift. Therefore, find out how much it will cost to secure an upgrade, a suite, or club level. And remember, many of the hotels that have frequent guest programs also offer confirmable upgrades for either no additional charge or only a nominal charge. Sometimes you can redeem points to obtain confirmable upgrades as well.

Quick Review

- Call directly to establish a relationship with hotel employees, and secure the best rooms at the lowest rates.
- When you secure a luxury room at a discount, be generous with the hotel representative who upgraded you.
- Make the flexibility of hotel rates work for you by exploring all available discounts.
- Book the lowest-priced room during the periods of low hotel occupancy in order to have the best chance of getting free or low cost upgrades.
- If you cannot secure a free upgrade, find out how much it would cost to upgrade to a more luxurious room. Often, the cost is nominal.

Preferential Treatment from Hotel Personnel

Just as flyers who seek preferential treatment should make friends with the airport gate agents, hotel travelers should acquaint themselves with the front desk representatives and the bell staff. A good relationship with the bell staff and front desk representatives can mean the most luxurious rooms in the hotel and the most valuable amenities. I have already discussed how the front desk staff can be instrumental in achieving the best room at the lowest price. Occasionally, however, a front desk representative will be unreceptive to your needs. When faced with this predicament, befriend the bellman when he escorts you to your room. If your room is unsatisfactory, ask the bellman to call the front desk in an attempt to arrange a new room.

On my first trip to the Ritz-Carlton Kapalua, the bellman

escorted me to a nice room but not a superb room. When I asked him about the various other rooms, he told me about their ocean front rooms and suites, and I asked him to call the front desk to request a change of rooms. While he was on the phone, I pulled two twenties from my pocket, conveying my intentions to tip him nicely. He was able to secure a beautiful ocean front room for the same price as the room I had reserved, and in return I tipped him $40, which seemed to make him very happy. Remember, when staff members are aware that they will be tipped generously, they will move mountains for you.

When dealing with front desk representatives or the bell staff, act as if it is an everyday occurrence to be treated in a preferential manner. Do not act like an unsophisticated tourist and gawk at the niceties of a fine hotel. Be complimentary, but not overtly excited. Without acting arrogant, anxious, or pretentious, behave as if it is no big deal to receive this preferential treatment. Remember, the very rich and famous expect luxury as their due, and so should you. Do, however, be genuinely appreciative of the people who treat you well.

The best time to negotiate an upgrade with a front desk representative is when they are not busy. Therefore, try to plan your arrival to the hotel at a time when all the other guests of the hotel are not trying to check in. For example, late afternoon is perhaps the busiest time for check-in, so if you know you are scheduled to arrive during this time period try to call the front desk in advance and request your upgrade before you even arrive at the hotel. If the front desk representative is not too busy, he or she will be more likely to listen to your needs, and search for the best room.

Additionally, when planning a trip for any special occasion or to a resort location, you should call the hotel directly and speak with the general manager to inform them of your impending arrival. Most likely, you will speak to the general manager's executive assistant, who will tag the reservation for preferential treatment. I have always found it beneficial to tell them about my enthusiasm for my impending visit and to mention any special occasions I might be celebrating. Anniversaries, weddings, or birthdays are good events to mention. This will usually yield you a fruit basket, champagne, or even a complimentary meal in their dining room. Moreover this can be an excellent time to request an upgrade if you have not already obtained one. By allying yourself with those who have the ability and willingness to provide you with special treatment, you will obtain the best rooms at the lowest price.

A story I read in CNN's *TravelGuide* on the Internet illustrates the importance of mentioning special occasions to hotel personnel when making your reservations. A Florida couple who spent their honeymoon back in 1948 at the Waldorf-Astoria Hotel in New York wanted to celebrate their 50th wedding anniversary there. The wife was in for a shock, however, when she learned that the least expensive room was $435—quite a difference from the $15 per night rate she and her husband had paid 50 years before. When she told the reservationist what her rate had been in that bygone era, the reservationist offered the couple their $15 per night rate plus tax for seven nights.

PRE-CHECK-IN AVAILABILITY

If you are unable to advantageously time your arrival, you should try to use the hotel's pre-check-in procedure. When you make your reservations, just ask the reservationist if this particular hotel offers this service. Some hoteliers permit all guests to do a pre-check-in on the day of arrival by calling an 800 number. This is usually a good idea for a couple of reasons. You can bypass the long lines to check in, and usually upon your request the pre-check-in phone representative will upgrade your room. Therefore, you will know in advance that you have been upgraded to luxurious accommodations. If you are unable to obtain an upgrade at the time of pre-check-in, you can follow one of the other methods to obtain an upgraded room, such as making friends with the bell staff.

Concierge Levels or Club Floors

Many hotels have special concierge levels or club floors. These special floors offer a variety of amenities, and you should always try to get upgraded to one of those rooms or negotiate access to that floor. Even if you have to pay a minimal fee, access to the concierge or club-level floors can actually save you money, especially when you are traveling with family members.

Here are some of the benefits of having access to the concierge or club level. There will be a dedicated concierge on the floor to assist with any of your needs. Unlike the concierges on the main floor, the concierges who work on these special floors can be very accommodating and greatly aid in making your travel experiences extra special and luxurious. When staying on these floors, you will also usually have access to complimentary breakfast, lunch, dinner, and drinks, which can result in tremendous savings. These floors usually offer coffee, juice, cereal, pastries, and fruit in the mornings, as well as a light meal service and free drinks throughout the day and early evening. In the late evening, they usually have some sort of bar set up in a quiet and private setting where you can relax and enjoy the extra amenities and privileges.

These special floors can clearly save you money, especially when you factor in the cost of room service or eating in the hotel's restaurant, and especially when you are upgraded to these floors without any additional charge. It has been my experience that the Ritz-Carlton offers one of the best concierge levels of all the hotel chains. They offer a lavish array of breakfast and lunch foods, and throughout the day light snacks and drinks are also available. For dinner they typically put out a classic buffet of light foods, and in the late evening they offer free drinks and sweets. The club area is also a great place to entertain guests and to be pampered by a very capable and attentive staff.

When traveling with your family, it is worth it to obtain at least one room on the concierge level, even if it means you have to pay extra for that room. If you have at least one room on the concierge floor, other members of your family will be able to partake in the free amenities provided on these floors. Even if you have to pay extra for one room, the money you save on meals and drinks for your family will more than make up for it.

When rooms are unavailable on the concierge or club level, a traveler who has established a loyal history with a hotel can discreetly ask the front desk representative or bellman to provide an access key to the floor. By giving a small tip in return for this access, you will find that the benefits are well worth it.

QUICK REVIEW

- Make friends with the front desk and bell staff. They can be instrumental in upgrading you to the most luxurious rooms for the same price or a bit more than an average room.

- Arrive at the hotel when the front desk will not be very busy. If you cannot arrange this, try to arrange for a pre-check-in and secure your upgrade in advance.
- Try to obtain an upgrade to a room on the concierge or club floors, or secure access to those floors if rooms are unavailable. Concierge and club levels can save you money on meals and offer a variety of luxurious amenities.

WHAT ABOUT TRAVEL AGENTS?

Once when traveling to London and Paris I used a travel agent to book my London hotel, but for the Paris part of my trip I confirmed and booked my own hotel. By far, Paris was a superior bargain. In London, I stayed at a shabby, overpriced hotel that was lacking in quality customer service. Consequently, I researched luxury hotels in the proximity and discovered that I could have stayed at the Four Seasons Hotel for the same price. On the other hand, in Paris I paid a low, discounted rate and stayed at a five-star luxury hotel located on the Avenue George V near the Champs Elysees. I was also upgraded to a top floor suite with a breathtaking view of the Eiffel Tower. This is the suite I described in Chapter One.

I have found that it is not an unusual situation to get an inferior deal when you book your hotel through a travel agent. They will often either book you in a second rate hotel, or they will confirm an overpriced rate in a finer hotel. Certainly, some travel agents are excellent at what they do and can be a valuable resource to you in your travels; however, it has been my experience that I can usually book a better deal on my own.

On a number of occasions I have asked a travel agent to book a hotel and was dissatisfied with the rate I was quoted. When I called the hotel directly, however, 90% of the time I was able to receive a lower rate through my own efforts. There is an important reason for this. Occasionally, some travel companies will offer bonuses to travel agents to promote their services. Therefore, it is possible that a travel agent could be working with their own commissions in mind rather than your best interests. Nonetheless, if you do decide to work with a travel agent, be sure to choose one wisely. I will cover this point in detail later in this book.

Despite the potential pitfalls of working with travel agents, they can be useful in providing information on destinations that are unfamiliar to you. However, by obtaining hotel directories, and with a computer and the Internet, you can research a multitude of travel ideas and destinations. This will enable you to construct a good package deal for yourself that not only saves you money, but also provides you with luxurious travels. How to go about your research is the subject of the next section.

RESEARCH CAN REALLY PAY OFF

Since the hotel industry has an unique pricing structure and methodology in determining room type, it is very important to do your homework. Most hotels have printed directories that list their properties and the specific amenities of each property. These books are a valuable reference tool when researching trips. I recommend that you obtain the directories for the Ritz-Carlton Hotels; the Leading Hotels of the World; and the publication for American Express Platinum Card holders, which is called the *Fine Hotels and Resorts Book*. The Ritz-Carlton's book includes listings of all of their properties and amenities, as well as the direct telephone numbers. The Leading Hotels of the World provides a listing of their elegant, four- and five-star hotels throughout the world. Although the Leading Hotels of the World do not have a frequent guest program, if you call their office and request it, they will set up an account that will track your guest history. The *Fine Hotels and Resorts Book* includes very upscale properties throughout the world and offers American Express Platinum Card holders exceptional rates.

If you have a computer and a modem, you can also have an array of useful travel tools at your fingertips. The United Connection is a free on-line software program from United Airlines which allows you to research and book reservations with over 30,000 hotels. Using this software allows you to view details on respective services and amenities, directions, points of interest, and reservation policies. You can also obtain useful travel information from numerous web sites on the Internet. In addition, some hotels have the ability to display graphically their properties over the computer. See the "Quick References" section in the back of this book for a listing of recommended web sites and available software.

PACKAGE DEALS

When researching your trips to resort locations, you will find that many hotel properties offer package deals. However, my advice is to stay away from most package deals. Very often, you will be able to piece together a better deal by utilizing the various discounts that are normally offered by hoteliers. Further, the front desk representatives are often instructed not to upgrade guests who are there on package deals. Because there are usually not any restrictions placed on upgrading guests with regular discounted rates, you will be more likely to receive an upgrade without the package deal.

Package deals often sound better than they actually are. To illustrate, there have been occasions in which I could book a room with a golf package for $200 more per day, but when I researched the golf rates I found out that they were only $50 per day. Therefore, the golf package would have cost me $150 more per day—certainly not a deal at all.

There are occasional exceptions to the package deal rule, however. Some resort locations, for example, offer good package deals, and these are worth considering. With a little research, you can find package deals that include a free car rental, meals, or sporting activities like golf, either for free or for only a nominal surcharge. Whenever I travel to a resort location, I often receive a free car rental, and by paying a slight surcharge of about $5 per day I am able to confirm a luxury upgrade to a car such as a Cadillac DeVille.

If You Don't Like Where You Are, Check Out

Do not be afraid to check out of an unsatisfactory property. This strategy is similar to the one I recommended when you are faced with having to fly another airline, and it is based on the principle of using the competitive nature of the market to your advantage. If you are faced with a stay in an unsatisfactory hotel property, I recommend that you do the following. First, call the front desk and tell them why you feel the hotel is not satisfactory. If they cannot improve the situation, then speak with the hotel's general manager. Remember, be polite and diplomatic; *never* act pushy or aggressive. Explain your dissatisfaction in a caring and concerned manner. However, if you are still dissatisfied, then check out of the hotel and go somewhere else. On some occasions you might be so initially dissatisfied that you decide it is not even worth your time to try and rectify the situation: checking out right away and going somewhere else will just seem like the right thing to do. This is a judgment call and your own personal decision.

Regardless of the procedure you follow, if you decide you wish to check out, do not stay even one night in an unsatisfactory hotel. Let the management know that you do not expect to be charged for your room. This is yet another reason to restrict your business to quality travel companies. They will almost always respect your wishes and either refund your money or not charge your credit card. Before checking out, however, do call another hotel in advance and ask to speak to the lead reservationist or the hotel manager. When speaking to these individuals, explain your situation. Generally, the staff at the new hotel will be very accommodating, as they will view this as an opportunity to win a new customer.

On one particular trip, I checked into the Ritz-Carlton in downtown Atlanta. Although I am a frequent guest of the Ritz-Carlton Hotels and regard them as one of the best luxury hoteliers, I was very disappointed with this particular hotel. When I was checking in, the front desk clerk was somewhat snappy and disdainful. Further, when I arrived at my room, it was not properly cleaned and the toilet was not flushed. Consequently, I called the Ritz-Carlton Buckhead, but I was told that they were full. However, when I asked to speak with the manager there and explained my dilemma to him, he offered me a discounted room on the club level. When I arrived at the property, he personally greeted me and had pre-arranged my check-in, which enabled me to proceed directly to my room. The following week I received a personal letter from the manager of the Ritz-Carlton downtown Atlanta property, offering me a complimentary visit on my next trip to Atlanta. I am happy to say that my next visit to the Ritz-Carlton Atlanta was superb. I was greeted immediately upon pulling up to the valet parking stand, the front desk clerk was a pleasure to speak with, and the upgraded room was immaculate.

On another occasion, I checked into the Hyatt Grand Champions in Palm Desert, California. To my chagrin, the level of service and quality had deteriorated since my last visit to this property. The front desk representative was extremely rude to me, and the hotel generally had a dingy, run-down feeling to it. As a result, I called the Stouffer's Esmeralda and explained the situation to the reservationist, who then placed me in a very nice room at a competitive rate.

Do not be afraid to utilize the competitive nature of the hotel industry to insure the most luxurious travels at a minimal cost. Above all, remember that the hotel you choose will significantly influence the overall satisfaction of your travels. A full service luxury hotel will provide you with a relaxing time-out from the stresses of your day. And when you are taking a vacation away from it all, a first class hotel will provide you with a relaxing atmosphere that will satisfy your every need and allow you to fully enjoy your time off.

Key Points

➢ ***Select a few hotel companies with which you will build a relationship, and cash in on your loyalty.***

Unlike most major airlines, there is inconsistency in quality and service, as well as location, among hotels. Therefore, to have the flexibility necessary to secure first class rooms at a discount every time, choose a select few hotel companies and stick with them.

- ***Take advantage of the tremendous flexibility in rates in the hotel industry.***
  Explore all available discounts, and be persistent.

- ***Take control of your hotel bookings and reap the biggest rewards.***
  Call directly, obtain upscale hotel directories, research the Internet, time your travels and check-ins. Be wary of package deals, and consider the benefits of making your own bookings instead of going through a travel agent.

- ***Make friends with the hotel staff.***
  Build relationships with front desk representatives and the bell staff; this can mean the difference between an average room and the most luxurious suite in the hotel.

- ***Seek access to the concierge or club levels.***
  These floors can save you money and are a luxurious oasis of amenities.

- ***Do not hesitate to check out if you are dissatisfied with a hotel.***
  Use the competitive nature of the hotel industry to your advantage.

7

The Mercedes Mentality

Driving a Premium Car at Discount Prices

On one trip to Hawai'i, I was able to pay for an economy class vehicle and still was treated like a VIP when I arrived at the airport. A rental agent immediately escorted me from the airport to the car rental facilities, ahead of all other renters and bypassing the long lines, to a Cadillac with the trunk popped open, the motor running, and the air conditioner cooling the car from the Hawaiian sun. This upgraded car and special treatment cost me no more than the price of an economy car.

On another recent occasion while traveling to Denver, I passed the Hertz rental counter. What I observed confirmed my opinion about the necessity of this book. Lined up were at least 50 people waiting to contract for their rental cars. Although I too was renting a Hertz car, I was permitted to bypass the chaos and proceed directly to the shuttle bus where I was the only passenger. Everyone else was still waiting in line. I was dropped off directly at my car where the engine was running and the trunk was open and ready to accept my baggage. And again, I had paid a discounted rate, yet received a complimentary upgrade to a luxury car. All in all, I was off to my meeting in less than five minutes, thoroughly enjoying the convenience of premium service.

The Importance of Upgraded and Luxury Car Rentals

The above experiences are not based on good fortune; they are based on a solid knowledge of how to obtain fast, upgraded car rentals and preferential treatment at discount prices. For me, hassle-free, low-cost upgraded and luxury car rentals are an everyday occurrence when I travel. And they can be for you.

Car rentals are a small yet important part of luxury travels. When you have the opportunity to drive a low-mileage, clean, upgraded vehicle such as a Cadillac DeVille, Lincoln Town Car, or Ford Explorer while on vacation, you will enhance your overall travel experience. And even if you have a chance to drive a roomier, four-door car that will accommodate your bags and passengers rather than a two-door compact on your business trips, it will make your journey that much more pleasant. After all, by now you are flying first class and staying in five-star hotels, so why not drive a more spacious or more luxurious car and receive preferential treatment, especially when you need not pay more than the average cost of an economy-size rental? Although there will be some occasions in which you might choose to pay the price of a mid-size rental in order to receive an upgrade to a higher class of car, the price difference is often negligible.

The benefits of knowing the secrets to renting cars also go beyond upgraded vehicles. In addition to saving money, you will be able to save time and the usual hassles associated with renting cars. No longer will you have to wait in those long rental lines, because you will be escorted directly to your car in advance of all other renters. And for the most part, obtaining a premium rental car at discount prices is a relatively simple procedure.

FREQUENT RENTER PROGRAMS

Similar to the airlines and hotel industry, major car rental companies track the rental history of their customers and offer preferential service to those who are loyal. Most of the major car rental companies are beginning to offer frequent renter programs that are similar to the airlines' frequent flyer programs and hotels' frequent guest programs. (See the "Quick Reference Section" in the back of this book for a list of these frequent renter programs.) By participating in these programs, renters can earn free car rentals, discounts, and upgrades. Alamo and Dollar were among the first to offer these programs, but soon the others followed. Therefore, similar to your approach with the airline and hotel industries, you will want to build a strong history of loyalty with select car rental companies.

A STRATEGY OF LOYALTY

When you are choosing a car rental company, you will want to follow a strategy similar to the one recommended for selecting hotels. In other words, instead of choosing just one car rental company, you will need to select at least two different companies. Like the hotel industry, you will find that rates and the availability of vehicles can vary somewhat according to location. However, for the most part car rental companies offer similar rates, and most major car rental companies have locations at airports throughout the world. There will be occasions when one company offers a grossly overpriced rate while another company offers a rate that is more reasonable. Likewise, on occasion you will find that one company will offer a special while another company might not. This is especially true when you rent in resort locations such as Hawaii or Orlando, ski resorts, and in Europe.

Therefore, to maintain flexibility, choose at least two rental companies—one as a primary company, the other as a secondary company—with which to build a loyal customer relationship. However, as in selecting hotels, you do not want to spread your business among too many companies, because you will want to establish a strong, loyal relationship. Furthermore, many of the car rental companies offer "partner points" with many of the airlines. So in addition to earning car rental points you can also accumulate points in your chosen airline's frequent flyer account. Therefore, consider choosing the car rental companies that offer points in your chosen airline's frequent flyer program. This will enable you to earn more points for first class upgrades and free tickets for family and friends. And not only will you earn additional airline miles, but your airline will also offer special car rental discounts and car upgrade opportunities.

I use Hertz as my primary car rental company and Avis as a secondary company. Both of these companies offer excellent frequent renter programs. My experience with these companies has been very favorable and, in my opinion, both of these companies offer attractive, new, clean, low-mileage cars along with very good customer service. They also offer enhanced services to frequent renters and have fairly good global coverage.

PREFERRED RENTER CLUBS

A few simple techniques make renting a car easier and permit you to bypass many of the common hassles associated with car rentals. Along with frequent renter programs, most major car rental companies offer what is known as preferred renter programs or clubs. When you belong to one of these preferred renter clubs, you are guaranteed better treatment simply by virtue of your membership. The good news is that you can join these programs at any time, even if you are a first time renter with that company. As for the car companies I use, Hertz has its "#1 Club Gold Program," and Avis has a "Preferred Renter Program." Members of these programs proceed directly to their cars, bypassing the long lines of renters, like the lines I saw at the Denver airport. In addition, car rental companies usually offer their preferred renters newer cars, special discounts, and automatic upgrades to one or more levels of car based upon availability. I will go into more detail on obtaining upgrades later in this chapter.

When renting from an airport location, you will usually need to take a shuttle bus from the airport terminal to the car rental location. However, when you are a member of these special clubs, the shuttle driver will take you directly to your car before any other passengers who might also be on the shuttle. Most Hertz rental locations also have a special canopy area that shields preferred customers from the weather. Furthermore, when you reach your car, it will have been pre-started, and you will find either the air conditioner or heater running to ensure a comfortable drive. And once you're in your car, all you need to do is show your driver's license to the representative at the exit gate and you're on your way.

In addition to the benefits you will receive at the airports, you will also be provided with a private 800-number staffed by well-trained representatives who usually are very accommodating and willing to meet your needs. Becoming a member of one of these car rental clubs is the best way to receive fast and courteous treatment from car rental companies.

How to Join Preferred Renter Clubs

Ordinarily, car rental companies will charge a fee for membership in their preferred renter clubs. Consequently, many consumers refrain from joining, because they believe that it is not worth the expense. What they do not realize, and what you, the well-informed traveler will now know, is that it is possible to join these clubs without paying a fee. By writing or calling your car rental company, you can usually get them to waive the membership fee. It makes sense for these companies to waive that fee, because in so doing they will secure you as a loyal patron of their company. Like most other service industry companies, the car rental industry is very competitive, and they want your business.

Here is how I got both Hertz and Avis to waive my annual membership fees. I called these companies and informed them that I was a frequent flyer of Delta Airlines (which is a mileage partner with both of these companies) and that I would give them my car rental business if they would waive my membership fee in their preferred renter clubs. As a result, both companies waived the fees, and each year they send me a letter stating that they have waived the fee for the upcoming year.

A special note: most of the rental companies that maintain frequent renter programs track your customer history or complete record exclusively on their central computer system. Consequently, most of the on-site rental locations will not have access to your complete rental history. However, your reservation will make note of your preferred renter club membership. Therefore, by virtue of being a member in these preferred renter clubs, the rental locations will treat you as a high frequency renter, even if you're not. I recommend researching the various car rental companies to see which ones will best meet your needs and contact them to become members in their preferred clubs. If for some reason your first choice does not offer you a free membership, which probably will not be the case, go to another company. Thankfully we are in a competitive market that offers a broad range of choices.

ELITE STATUS

In addition to the preferred renter clubs that are available to the general public, car rental companies also offer a very elite level of service that is reserved for CEOs and business executives who can influence the car rental decisions of their companies. If you happen to fall into this category, do look into this status. These elite renters are greeted at the airport gate, escorted directly to their car waiting curbside at the airport, and are always given the best car on the lot. Upon their return, these members are escorted directly back to the airport. However, this type of elite status is difficult to obtain. When I called the corporate office of Hertz to inquire into their Platinum status, they informed me that if I qualified, they would know. Their policy is to contact those whom they feel deserve this status.

QUICK REVIEW

- A better car will enhance your overall travel experience.
- Like choosing hotel companies, select at least two car rental companies (a primary company and a secondary company) with which you will build a loyal partnership.

- Join the frequent renter programs, preferred rental clubs, receive preferential treatment, and get your club membership fees waived.

Be Persistent About Obtaining the Best Rate

After you have researched and selected the car rental companies with which you wish to do business, gained access to their preferred renter clubs and, if available, joined their frequent renter programs, you will want to obtain the highest level of car at the lowest possible rate. Again the car rental industry parallels the hotel industry very closely. When searching for the best price and highest level of car, you will need to call the car rental companies directly, sometimes making several phone calls to get the kind of car at the rate you want. Similar to calling hotels, it is not uncommon to speak with one rental agent and be offered one rate and then call back a few minutes later and get another rate.

Seek Out All Available Discounts

The best method of getting the lowest rate is to seek out and utilize all available discounts. Similar to the hotel industry, car rental companies also offer a myriad of discounts. Discounts will range from corporate discounts to those affiliated with airlines and hotels, so ask for all possible discounts. Often I have found that AAA has special rates with many of the car rental agencies.

UPGRADES THROUGH YOUR OTHER TRAVEL PARTNERS

Frequently, you will receive car rental upgrade certificates or special code numbers from your airline or other travel partners. When you do have one of these certificates or code numbers, make sure to mention it to the reservation agent, so that they can note it in your electronic record. For example, as a Delta Airlines Platinum Medallion member, I have a "PC Code" that allows for me to receive special car rental upgrades. But be aware that some of the agents may not know how to enter this code into your reservation. When I encounter this kind of situation, I just call back and the next agent usually knows how.

CASH IN ON YOUR LOYALTY

As previously stated, usually if you are a member of a car rental company's preferred renter club and/or frequent renter program, you will automatically be upgraded one or more car levels based upon availability. However, it helps to remind the reservation agent that you would like to request an upgrade. Ask what kinds of upgraded vehicles are available in inventory, and put in a request for the vehicle you want. Types of cars vary according to location. If you arrive at your car and would prefer a different model, you can also, subject to availability, successfully request a change of vehicle at the car rental lot.

UPGRADES AT RESORT LOCATIONS

Usually the only locations in which you can confirm a luxury car rental in advance are resort locations. This is because many car rental agencies at resort locations have an inventory of luxury vehicles that regularly go unrented, especially during the off-season, since most people do not want to pay more for a luxury car and are unfamiliar with how to obtain one without additional cost. With this in mind, make sure that when you travel to a resort, you utilize your established relationship with the car rental company to obtain the highest level vehicle without additional cost. And again, this is yet another reason to adhere to the contrarian strategy of luxury travel.

If you are traveling to a resort and were unable to confirm a luxury rental when you made your reservation or would like a higher level luxury car, go to the special line or lounge designated for members of their club, identify yourself as a club member, and express your disappointment with the vehicle allotted to you. Try to speak with the manager or the lead person of the car rental location and request an upgrade.

Another way to increase your probability of being upgraded if you were unable to confirm one through the reservation service is to consider calling the on-site manager in advance of your arrival. Tell the manager that you rent often from their company and would appreciate any special accommodations they can provide. This technique is especially helpful for those times when you want to avoid having to take any additional steps to secure an excellent car. It has been my experience that most on-site managers are very accommodating and will usually upgrade you to a higher level of car, especially when you are a member in their preferred renter program.

Another thing to consider doing if you are traveling to a resort location is to ask the hotel where you will be staying if they offer a package rate, which might include a rental car. As we saw in the previous chapter, you can sometimes package a rental car into your hotel reservation and for a few additional dollars receive an upgraded class of car. If your hotel will not arrange to upgrade your car, call the rental agency; in most cases they will accommodate you.

NON-SMOKING CARS

As a side note, no matter where you travel you will increase your odds for a newer, cleaner car when you request a non-smoking car. This is a necessity if you are a non-smoker, for there is nothing worse than a car that emits stale cigarette odors from the air conditioner. Further, you will increase your chances for an upgrade, because if a non-smoking car (the most requested car type) is unavailable in the class of service you booked, you will be upgraded to accommodate your non-smoking needs.

CHECK OUT THE DIFFERENCE IN COST

It is also worthwhile to look into the difference in price between an economy size rental, a midsize car, a full size, and a luxury car. Customarily, the difference in price is only a few dollars a day, and sometime it will even cost less to rent a higher level of car! I recall while planning a trip to Hawai'i, I was quoted a mid-size car rate of $250 per week. However, upon further inquiry, I found out that there was a special luxury rate of only $215 per week. Therefore, I was able to confirm a Cadillac, which is three to four levels above a midsize car, for $35 per week less than I would have paid for a midsize.

Likewise, one day when I was quoted the usual rate with Hertz for a midsize rental car, I asked what my rate for a full size rental would be. *It was the same.* Then I asked about the rate for an economy size and again it was the same. As a result, I now book a full size car at the same price as the economy, but since I am always upgraded at least one class size because of my preferred renter club membership, *I am now upgraded based on a full size rental.* Very often the rate difference between the class sizes is inconsequential, a few dollars a day. However, most people ask for the lowest price rental, which is the economy size, and fail to inquire further. *Be sure to investigate all possible rate options.*

On another occasion while traveling in Europe, I found it necessary to travel to Frankfurt and Brussels. After researching the fares for inter-European flights, I decided that it would be more economical to drive. (Besides, if you have ever had the good fortune to drive the autobahn, then you know what fun that can be.) While researching rates and availability of cars, I came across a "Drive Europe" special that allowed me to rent a luxury car for what I would normally pay in the U.S. for a midsize car. Upon further questioning, I found that I could upgrade to a premium Mercedes Class for less than ten dollars extra per day, and that rate included insurance, whereas the lower rate did not. Even with the upgrade to the Mercedes, my rate was effectively lower than a midsize car in America. For this excellent price, I was able to drive a beautiful Mercedes Benz, which was equivalent to the U.S. version of an E-320, on the pristine, open road between Frankfurt and Brussels. Pure pleasure!

To obtain your own upgraded and luxury car rentals at a discount, remember to be persistent and inquire about all available special offers and discounts, price differences between luxury cars and lower classes of cars, prices of all available upgrades, and whether insurance can be included in the price.

You Deserve the Best

As with all other aspects of your luxury travels, be a stickler for quality. Any time you arrive at your car and it does not meet your standards, let the manager know. If the car is not clean, has high mileage, or is not the type of car you want, request a different car. I have never had my request to change a car denied. Of course, use this technique judiciously. For example, if you are only using the car to drive a short distance to a meeting and then back to the airport, it is probably not worth your time to exchange your car. Just be sure that the next time you make a reservation, mention that you were not satisfied with the last car, and most likely the reservationist will make a note to upgrade the current rental for you.

CAR RENTAL INSURANCE

Another thing to bear in mind in terms of cost is car insurance. Before renting a car, check with your personal automobile insurance to see what type of insurance coverage it provides for rental cars. Likewise, ask your credit card company about this; many will provide rental car insurance coverage when you use their card for car rentals. If your credit card does not offer this coverage, consider using a card that does. Many of the "Gold Cards" provide coverage while renting a car. These options will allow you to save money by refusing the expensive coverage that rental companies aggressively promote. Unless I am renting internationally, I refuse the rental companies' insurance coverage, because I find that I am well covered on my own. However, do take extra care to check what coverage you have outside the United States, as it can often be difficult to resolve problems overseas.

Renting a car is one element of many that enhances your overall luxury travel experience. So treat yourself well, receive preferential service from car rental companies, and drive the finest cars available at discounted prices.

Key Points

- ***Add another pleasurable dimension to your travels through car rentals.***
  Drive a spacious, upgraded car or premium luxury vehicle, and get the most enjoyment from your time on the road.

- ***Follow a strategy similar to the hotels.***
  Choose a primary and a secondary car rental company; this will allow you to maintain loyalty while having the flexibility to insure the best car at the lowest price.

- ***Join special preferred renter clubs free of charge.***
  These special clubs will provide you with preferential treatment, discounts, and upgrades. Usually by calling your rental company and pledging your loyalty, they will waive the fee for joining their clubs.

- ***Join frequent renter programs.***
  These programs will allow you to earn points that can be traded in for upgrades and discounts, and often they will earn you points in your airline frequent flyer programs.

- ***Seek out all available discounts and special offers, and inquire into the price difference for an upgraded car.***
  Ask the right questions, be persistent, and you will be rewarded with luxury cars at discounted prices.

- ***Check your personal auto insurance and credit cards for rental insurance.***
  Often you'll find you are covered. However, some companies offer only domestic coverage. When renting overseas, it may be wisest to pay for the rental company's insurance coverage or negotiate it as part of the rental package.

8

Travel Mishaps

Turning Misfortune Into Fortune

While staying at the Hilton Towers in Chicago, an early morning meeting required that I leave the hotel shortly before 6:30 a.m. During this stay I had been upgraded to the concierge level, but the lounge that offered complimentary coffee and breakfast to concierge-level guests did not open until 6:30 a.m. When I approached the lounge at 6:25, I saw a hotel employee preparing to open up the lounge. Speaking through the closed door, I politely asked if I could have a cup of coffee. But the employee refused, brusquely informing me that they would not open until 6:30.

Later that day, I told the hotel's general manager what had transpired that morning. He was so apologetic that he waived all my charges for my current stay. In addition, he offered me a complimentary stay on my next trip to Chicago.

Even the Best Make Mistakes

When travel service companies make mistakes, the knowledgeable traveler can turn misfortune into fortune. Most upscale travel service companies strive to maintain a credible reputation for providing exceptional service. Even with the best travel partners, however, you will experience isolated incidents in which they do not meet their usual high standards. Consequently, any time a dissatisfied customer has a legitimate complaint, quality-oriented companies will usually go out of their way to make amends to maintain their reputation. The circumstances of your mishap and the courteous manner in which you present your case will usually dictate what compensation the company chooses to offer. This chapter will show you how to capitalize on but not exploit travel mishaps.

FIRST, DO YOUR PART TO AVOID UNSATISFACTORY TRAVELS

Before I get into the specifics of how to turn travel misfortune into fortune, it is important to stress that the responsibility for the quality of your travels starts with you. Over the years I have become extremely knowledgeable about the advantages and disadvantages of Delta Airline's various routes and flights. I know what planes fly on what routes, how many seats there are in the first class cabin, and what flights will generally have a heavy load of passengers. Out of Orange County, where I live, Delta has relatively few flights; therefore I have made it a point to study what flights are best suited for my needs and opt for those first. Furthermore, I know which flights offer the best opportunity for upgrades and which flights offer me the best chance to clear a wait list for first class.

Also, while you might assume that all first class cabins are created equal, they are not. On one of the routes that I regularly fly, the first leg of the journey is on an older model plane with only eight first class seats, which are quite roomy and comfortable. On the second leg of the journey, however, the newer aircraft has a first class cabin with twelve smaller and less comfortable seats. Consequently, I've found that if I take an earlier flight on that route, I am able to fly both legs of the journey on planes offering the roomier and more comfortable first class seats. In addition, you will find that some flights offer drinks and snacks rather than full meals, even in the first class cabin. This is why being a student of your chosen airline is very important. Get to know the specific seating configurations and cabin service (meals and movies) offered on the planes that fly particular routes. This information is usually available in the airline's schedule book, frequent flyer on-board magazines, and on the web sites of some airlines. You can also ask the reservationist for this information as well. By developing a thorough understanding of your travel partner you can leverage your knowledge and take an alternate route or flight that would offer you a more comfortable environment.

As you build your relationship with your air carrier or with any of your other travel partners, you will develop your own personal strategy for optimizing your first class travels. The more you become familiar with the particular idiosyncrasies of your travel partners, the less chance there will be for disappointments and mishaps. However, even the most carefully planned travels with the highest quality travel partners can occasionally result in a disappointing or unsatisfactory experience. When this happens, there are specific techniques you can use in order to receive compensation for your dissatisfaction.

COMPLAINTS

Complain only when you have a legitimate concern. It is important to point out that although quality travel companies want to appease dissatisfied customers, *you as a customer have a responsibility not to take advantage of these companies' efforts to maintain goodwill.* Remember that you are building long-term relationships with companies and repeatedly doing business with them. Therefore, if you regularly make vague, unreasonable, or false complaints, these companies will eventually learn to be skeptical of your motives and will be less likely to try to make amends. With this in mind, choose carefully the people to whom you complain, and *complain only when you have a legitimate concern.*

Know what to reasonably expect from a legitimate complaint. When voicing your dissatisfaction, you should have a clear idea of what type of compensation you are seeking; however, I like to first give the travel company representative an opportunity to specify the form of amends they would like to offer. Then, if I feel their offer is insufficient, I will suggest what I think is fair. I feel that it is a good idea first to allow the company to make their offer, because very often quality companies will offer more than you would even think to ask for. The above story about my stay at the Hilton Towers in Chicago is a case in point. Because I was not able to get a coffee five minutes early, the charges for my current stay were waived, and I was offered a complimentary future stay. Although I was very appreciative of the manager's offer, I was frankly surprised at the extent to which he went to make amends. But again, this is why it pays to spend your travel dollars exclusively on quality companies. They have a reputation to maintain and will go to great lengths to do so.

Another reason to allow the company to make the first offer of compensation is to avoid coming across as a person who is out to take advantage of the situation. However, when you do find it necessary to make a specific request, ask only for what is appropriate for the mistake.

Quick Review

- Quality companies strive to maintain their reputation for quality, which is why they will want to make amends if you are dissatisfied.
- Learn the idiosyncrasies of your travel partners in order to avoid unsatisfactory travel experiences.
- Do voice your complaints, but only when you have a legitimate concern. Do not take advantage of a company's goodwill.
- Keep in mind what you think would be fair recompense for your dissatisfaction, but allow the company to make the first offer of amends.

Ask, and You Shall Receive

Today's traveler has a lot to complain about. There are increasing lines at the airports; planes are more crowded than they have been in years; and hotels, car rental agencies, and cruise lines tend to overbook. My friend was traveling with her two young daughters when their plane experienced mechanical difficulties. After sitting on the hot and sweltering runway for two hours, the plane finally returned to the gate. When she was finally able to locate airline representatives, they said that they could book her on a flight to her destination that left in six hours, offering nothing more than coach seats. She diplomatically told the agent that this offer was unacceptable. What she believed would be fair, she said, was a hotel near the airport, vouchers for dinner and breakfast, phone calls to call home, and a flight on a competitor's airline in the first class cabin. The agent agreed to fulfill all of her requests. And when my friend returned home, she wrote a letter to that airline and received free vouchers for flights in the future. Remember, although you can profit by complaining, you should only do so when it is legitimate.

On the other hand, my friend Carol wished she had read this book before her mishap at Denver International Airport. Carol was about to fly home from a business meeting when her flight was delayed because United Airlines did not have anyone to fly the plane. When United finally located a flight crew, the pilots refused to fly because they had already worked too many hours. Three hours later, Carol was still stranded. Eventually, all the flights to her destination were canceled and she had to wait until the next day for a flight. When the airline announced that the flights were canceled, they also announced that they did not have any hotels available for the stranded passengers. So they handed out airline blankets and pillows. When Carol finally arrived at her destination the next morning, the nightmare continued. To retrieve her bags, which had been sent ahead the day before, she had to wait in one line to confirm that her bags were there. Then she had to wait in another line to actually get her bags. With all of these mishaps, she was not offered any compensation. However, after speaking with me about it, she sent a letter of complaint to United Airlines.

If you find yourself stranded at the airport due to flight cancellation or mechanical difficulty, your highest priority will be to get on another flight. The quickest way to accomplish this is to head to the nearest pay phone or use your cellular phone to call the airline's 800-number reservation service. If you are a member of the airline's private lounge, you can head there for help as well. These are much more efficient alternatives to waiting with a lot of other stranded passengers in the long customer service lines. If you feel that compensation for your inconvenience is warranted, you can then talk to the gate agent or write to the airline.

Consider What a Company Can and Cannot Reasonably Do

Although the best companies want to provide an exceptional level of customer satisfaction, bear in mind that these companies also need to maintain profitability. Consequently, they cannot give away the store, so do consider what a company or its representatives can and cannot reasonably do. To illustrate, I was checking into a hotel and requested that the hotel provide me with points in my frequent flyer account. I also requested points in the hotel's frequent guest program. (At the time, this particular hotel chain was running a promotion that offered additional amenities based on the number of nights you stayed within a given time period. More importantly, I wanted to continue building my loyal customer history with the hotel.) However, the front desk clerk to whom I had made my request said that she could not give me points in both my frequent flyer and frequent guest programs. I explained that this was a perfectly legitimate request that I am granted all the time, but she insisted it was not possible. When I politely asked that she check with her manager, she did, and she found out that what I had requested was allowable. Then, she not only apologized for giving me a hard time, she also upgraded me to a suite. This is why it is crucial to know what you can and cannot legitimately request.

Consider this quite different scenario. Perhaps you've arrived at your hotel late, and due to an error made by the hotel, they overbooked and have absolutely no vacancies. When you express your displeasure, however, the hotel does offer you a free night's stay at a comparable hotel and a free night at one of their own hotels at a later date. In this case, it would be unreasonable and unproductive to argue and demand a room in that hotel for that evening. It would also be unfeasible to expect the hotel to make a guest leave a room.

Again, make sure your complaint has merit, and seek compensation that is appropriate to the circumstances. For instance, if an airline has delayed your flight for one hour due to mechanical reasons, you should probably just go with the flow. But if it is delayed for five hours, you might voice your concern and ask for a free ticket, first class upgrade certificates, or an earlier flight on another airline. Likewise, if your room service meal arrived thirty minutes late, you should not expect the hotel to offer you a free weekend in their presidential suite; however, it is not unreasonable to expect the hotel to adjust your room service charges.

GO UP THE CHAIN OF COMMAND

If you are dissatisfied, try to deal with the problem immediately, and most often your dissatisfaction will be dealt with on the spot. You will also want to be sure that you are dealing with someone who has the willingness, authority, and desire to see to your needs. It is useless and a waste of your efforts to try to resolve a bad situation with someone who has neither the insight nor the authority to resolve the dilemma. You will want to avoid those individuals and seek out the ones who have the attitude and wherewithal to help you. On an airline, speak with the lead flight attendant or the gate supervisor; on a tour, speak to the tour leader; on a cruise, seek out the steward; and at a hotel, speak to the general manager or his or her assistant. (There will be more specific advice about voicing complaints at hotels in the next section.) Don't, however, jump the chain of command unless you find it necessary; whenever possible, start with the source of the problem. If that does not yield the desired results, ask for that person's manager. And if that still does not get results, speak to that person's supervisor. Simply put, if the individual you are working with is unable or unwilling to assist you, seek out someone of higher authority. Do, however, remember to be diplomatic; never act pushy or overbearing.

QUICK REVIEW

- If what a company offers you in terms of amends is unacceptable, ask for what you think is fair and appropriate to the circumstances.
- Seek appropriate compensation for your dissatisfaction, but bear in mind what is reasonable and feasible for the company to do. Do not be unreasonable in your requests.
- Deal with the problem immediately, and whenever possible, begin by voicing your complaint to the person through whom you encountered the problem.
- In any case, seek out someone with the willingness, authority, and desire to help you, and ask for a supervisor if you still are not satisfied.

THE BEST HOTELS ARE QUICK TO RESPOND TO CUSTOMER COMPLAINTS

When voicing your complaints to hotel industry companies in particular, you will find that they have great leeway in the amenities that they can offer you. A seemingly inconsequential event voiced to the right person will reap surprisingly big rewards. Therefore, when you are at a hotel, if the person immediately assisting you is unwilling or unable to make amends, try to deal with the most senior employee on the premises. If you are unable to speak with the General Manager or the Property Manager, try to speak with at least the Assistant Manager. The best hotels are very quick to respond to guests making a complaint. The last thing they want is a guest ranting and raving in the lobby, in front of other guests. That's the last thing you want to do as well. Whenever you make a complaint at a hotel—or at any travel company—make sure to do so calmly and courteously. Be understanding enough to realize that mishaps do occur from time to time.

Another thing to keep in mind is that it always gives you an edge when you approach your hotel complaint from a position of a loyal customer who cares about the overall service of the hotel. You could say, for example, "I have stayed here in the past, and on this occasion I am somewhat disappointed." Or you might say, "Is this hotel going through some changes, because…" Or you could also say, "In the past while staying at one of your hotels, I never had this kind of problem; is something wrong here?" If you are unable to meet and express your displeasure to the hotel's manager during your stay, you can also write a letter after checking out. In most instances, the manager will respond and usually offer you a free night's stay.

A friend of mine and his wife and children were on a return trip from Paris with a one-day stopover in Seattle, Washington. At the last minute, they rearranged their travel plans in order to stay at the airport Hilton Hotel. Unbeknownst to him at the time he made his reservation, that particular Hilton was due for extensive improvements. Their non-smoking room smelled of tobacco and the hallway carpets were badly stained. They were, however, too tired to complain at the time. The next day, my friend's wife approached the hotel manager and told him that their experience was atypical of the Hilton chain. Without another word, the manager zeroed out their charges, apologized for the shabby demeanor of the hotel, told her about the new improvements taking place, and invited her and her family back for a complimentary visit after the renovations were complete.

It is very easy for hotels to offer compensation for your dissatisfaction, because—believe it or not—so few people actually complain. A recent column in *The New York Times* quoted one Hyatt official who estimated that only one in every hundred people complain, and more times than not, that one person never asks the hotel to make specific amends. However, according to this article, those who do complain can expect the following:

Complaints that might merit a free night's stay:

- A closed pool
- The sound of a jackhammer in the early morning
- No beach on the hotel property when the brochure showed pictures of a beach
- False fire alarms throughout the night
- No hot water
- Hotel under construction, causing inconveniences
- King-size bed is replaced with twin beds

Other annoyances that might merit a free meal or drinks:

- Hotel employee is rude
- Excessive wait for a room
- Spa is closed
- Being stranded in the lobby without a bellhop
- A nonsmoking room reeks of cigarette smoke

QUICK REVIEW

- If a hotel employee does not offer to make amends, make an effort to speak with the most senior management person on the premises.
- Always be calm and courteous, and realize that mishaps do occur from time to time.
- Approach your complaint from the position of a loyal customer who cares about the overall service of the hotel.
- Hotels are in a position to offer you a broad scope of amenities as compensation.

CHOOSE YOUR BATTLES

At this point, it would be wise to make mention of employee attitudes. As you travel, you will come across some employees who have an excellent attitude, while other employees might be having a rough day or perhaps are not suited for a customer service job. On one occasion, I was traveling in the state of Washington and needed to take a carrier with whom I rarely fly. Prior to the flight, I called the airline's marketing department and asked if they would upgrade me, which they did. On my outbound flight, I was upgraded without a hitch. However, when I checked in for my return flight, the counter agent gave me a boarding pass for coach. Without looking at the boarding pass, I approached the gate agent to show my ID and asked her if I had an aisle seat in first class. She looked at me and sneered back, "You are not in first class." I replied that I was and asked her to double check. "No," she replied, "you are not in first class. Go to customer service if you want help." (By the way, I was the only person in line at the gate counter.)

In a somewhat foul mood, I went to customer service and asked for help. The woman there cheerfully informed me that I was issued the wrong boarding pass and took care of the problem. In this situation, I did not even brother to seek any amends from the company, because it is unlikely I will be flying with them again. This brings up another important point: *Pick and choose your battles*. Sometimes, it's just not worth it to complain. Your best payback is to not do any more business with them.

My advice is this: When you come across someone with a poor attitude, whether it's an airline employee or an employee of another kind of travel company, your best bet is to deal with someone else. The goal here is not to get into a clash with anyone. If you are on the phone with a difficult person, just end the call politely, call back, and get a more civil representative. Before you end your call with an unpleasant employee, however, do try to get that person's name, and when you speak to the new representative, tell them that you were just dealing with an unpleasant person. This will usually encourage the new representative to be extra nice to you. If you are dealing with someone unpleasant face to face, kindly ask to speak to that person's supervisor. And when the supervisor arrives, always be civil, no matter how upset you are. This will make you look blameless, and the supervisor will work harder to assist you. But remember if you are unpleasant, most people will be less than willing to go out of their way for you.

Do All You Can to Resolve Airline Complaints Before Boarding

When voicing a complaint to airline industry companies, keep the following in mind: if you are dealing with an airline representative over the phone and are not satisfied, ask for customer service or the supervisor of the representative who is unwilling to meet your needs. And always try to get that person's name. If you complain while at the airport, you might try first to resolve your dilemma with the counter agent. If that is not successful, or if the counter agent does not have the authority or willingness to resolve the situation, then go higher. This probably will be a gate agent supervisor. You might also try to resolve your dilemma in the private members' lounge; usually those representatives provide a high level of quality service.

If you are on the plane, you will want to seek out the highest-ranking flight attendant, usually referred to as the flight coordinator. As always, it will also help if you mention how loyal a customer you are. If the situation warrants, ask to speak with the plane's captain. However, if you complain to the plane's captain, be extremely conscious of speaking very politely. Also be cognizant of the captain's willingness to listen to you. If the captain is too busy or unwilling to listen, do not push the matter; wait until you are off the plane. Captains have a great deal of authority to resolve your problems, but if you are perceived as being the least bit rude or pushy with them, they will ignore your complaint or worse: you could be in trouble.

There are potential dangers to you in voicing a complaint to any airline employee while on board a flight: if anyone on the flight crew perceives you as interfering with their duties, you could be liable for a fine by the FAA or even find yourself strong-armed by airline security once the plane lands. Therefore, proceed with extreme caution when on board the plane. If the flight crew is unwilling or too busy to assist you, *do not pursue the matter on board.* Wait until you are off the plane and speak to customer service. If you push an issue with a captain or any flight crew member, you could find yourself answering to the FAA.

The Rewards of Being Bumped

Here is an interesting perspective on another sort of travel mishap—getting bumped from an airline flight. Being asked to give up your seat on an overbooked flight can be seen as an inconvenience; however, it can also work to your advantage. My friend Blake, who frequently flies in connection with his work for the government, was booked at the last minute on a Continental flight. Unfortunately, he did not have an advance opportunity to secure an upgrade to first class. So when the gate agent came back into the crowded and cramped coach section to ask if anyone would be willing to give up his seat, Blake readily volunteered. In return, Blake was offered a first class seat on a flight one hour later and two vouchers for free future flights.

Getting bumped can reap valuable rewards, and according to the Department of Transportation, the number of bumped passengers is on the rise. In one recent three month period, American Airlines bumped 50% more passengers than the same period the year before. Delta Airlines asked 45% and 55% more passengers to volunteer their seats in the first and second quarters of the same year. If you are bumped, you can typically expect to receive a voucher worth a couple of hundred dollars for a delay of a few hours, and a voucher worth $400 or more for a longer delay. However, as in Blake's case, compensation can be negotiated, leading to multiple tickets, cash, upgrade certificates, and more. When a gate agent enters the plane asking for volunteers is when the airline is the most desperate and when the most lucrative incentives will be offered.

The same family who had the poor night at the Hilton in Seattle voluntarily gave up their five seats on an overbooked Chicago-to-Paris flight. For the minor inconvenience of spending one very pleasant night at the Hilton, they were rewarded with ticket vouchers worth $2,500. In addition, the gate agent called their Paris hotel to inform them of the family's delay.

Getting bumped can also be a good strategy for flying first class if you were otherwise unsuccessful in obtaining a first class upgrade. Just make sure that as part of your compensation, you receive a first class seat on the next flight. By the way, if you are already booked in first class, you will not usually be asked to give up your seat.

Your chances of being bumped are greater if you book your flight during a peak time (Thursday, Friday, or Sunday between 3 p.m. and 7 p.m.). If you're traveling on a route that has frequent departing flights, ask to be booked on a flight that is already full, but unless you want to risk spending the night in that city, make sure there's a later flight. Some travelers enjoy the fruits of being bumped several times on the same trip by traveling during peak periods, on busy holidays, and by volunteering to be bumped. Incidentally, if you did not get a boarding pass when you received your ticket, you have a better chance of being bumped. However, to be eligible for full compensation, you must be checked in at least 20 minutes before the flight. Finally, if your airline places you on another airline's flight as compensation, make sure to request that you receive "base mileage" credit on your chosen airline for that flight. This will help you continue to build your loyal customer status with your airline.

Nothing But the Best

The aforementioned techniques for voicing complaints with the airlines and hotels can be applied to a broad range of situations. These methods will also be effective if you experience trouble with a car rental company or a cruise line. Virtually any time a quality travel company fails to meet your standards, these strategies will work to correct the mishap. In fact, if you effectively voice a legitimate complaint to any type of service-related company, you can receive appropriate compensation. For example, if a retailer fails to deliver your new television set on time, you can usually negotiate a free service contract or voucher for free merchandise. I once received a $50 store certificate when Circuit City failed to properly deliver my television. Or if a restaurant does not properly prepare your meal, speak up in a courteous and respectful manner. In fact, today's diners at all levels of restaurants are more likely to send their plates back if they are not satisfied. One restaurateur, Ron Trimberger, was quoted in *The Wall Street Journal* as saying that more customers today "know what they want and what they don't want." This trend is true of all industries, particularly in the travel industry. Today's consumers have a wide array of choices available to them, and companies know that dissatisfied consumers will simply take their business elsewhere.

As a consumer on a quest for first class travel, you have the right to expect and receive nothing less than the best. If a travel company fails to meet your (and its) high standards, inform the highest-ranking official in a professional and caring manner. This will always insure that you maintain your own high standards of traveling in an ultra-luxurious mode.

Key Points

➢ ***Understand that quality companies strive to maintain their reputation for quality.***

This allows the savvy traveler the opportunity to benefit

when a quality travel company makes an error or otherwise fails to maintain its high standards.

➢ ***Do not take advantage of a travel company's goodwill.***
It is unwise and unethical to exploit the good intentions of quality travel companies. Taking advantage will prevent you from building a solid, long-term relationship with those companies, because eventually those companies will lose interest in serving you.

➢ ***Restrain your eagerness to initially request a specific form of amends.***
Allow the company's representative to make the first offer of amends. If you make a preemptive request, you might come across as trying to exploit the situation. Quite often the company's offer will exceed what you might have requested.

➢ ***Seek compensation that is appropriate and reasonable for the mistake and the circumstances.***
When you do request specific compensation for your dissatisfaction, ask for something that is reasonable and fair. Do not request a free week at a hotel for late room service.

➢ ***Don't waste your time wrangling with someone who has a poor attitude. Instead, seek out another representative (or a competing company) who is willing to help you.***
When voicing pre- or post-flight complaints to an airline, go up the chain of command until you are satisfied. However, be extremely careful to avoid being troublesome when you are in-flight. There can be serious consequences.

9

Tips on Tips

Knowing Who to Tip, How to Tip, and When to Tip

While on a business trip in Phoenix, Arizona, my friend John learned how a small investment in tipping can pay big dividends. He was keen to play golf during his one day off, but was unable to secure a tee time at any local golf course. By the time he called the bell desk to inquire about laundry service, he'd resigned himself to giving up the idea. When the bell person came to his room to pick up his laundry, John mentioned his disappointment about being unable to play golf. He also tipped the bell person a few dollars for tending to his laundry needs. Less than five minutes later, this same bell person called John's room to announce he'd not only arranged a tee time at John's preferred golf course, but had also arranged a rate that was less than half the usual price. John gratefully tipped this entrepreneurial bell person an additional $20 and was treated like a king for the remainder of his stay.

Tips are an Investment

Many of the employees who work in the travel industry derive the majority of their income from tips. Consequently, they have a vested interest in providing the best service possible, since a higher quality of service insures that they receive better tips. Therefore, when you tip and how you tip will be important to these employees, who will go out of their way to give you preferential service. Look at your tips as an investment in your quest for luxury travel. If you tip wisely, you will be able to gain benefits far in excess of the average traveler. This does not mean you need to be extravagant in order to receive preferential treatment, but you do need to be prudent and perceptive.

It Pays to Tip a Little Extra for Preferential Service

The derivation of the word "tips" is "To Insure Prompt Service," but I like to think it means "To Insure Preferential Service." Thus a fundamental principle in traveling like the rich and famous is that in many situations it will be necessary to tip a little extra to insure preferential treatment. Although you might usually think of tips as a reward you give to a service employee for having provided you with superior service, in some cases your tips are given in anticipation of the future preferential service they are about to provide. That's where the derivation of the word "tips" comes into play—you are insuring the high quality of service you have come to expect. However, as you will see later in the chapter, when you are requesting special services or amenities, such as an upgraded room or access to a club floor, you should hold off on your tip until after you receive the desired service or preferential treatment in return.

When should you tip in anticipation of future preferential service? It is generally a good practice to do this when you first arrive at a hotel and drive up to the valet parking stand or after a bellman first brings your bags to your room or performs a service such as delivering your laundry to your room. By simply adding a couple of extra dollars to the customary tip indicated in the chart at the end of this chapter, that staff person whom you tipped well the first time will be more likely to go out of his or her way to accommodate you if you should make special requests thereafter.

Hotels are a common place where you will utilize this technique to insure preferential service during your stay. Since hotels are the places in which you will spend most of your tip money, a good deal of this chapter will be devoted to advice on hotel tipping. It has been my experience that in most hotels you will receive the most preferential service from the bell staff, valet parking staff, and front desk representatives. Consequently, I recommended that you invest your tips in these employees in particular. In return, these individuals will go out of their way to enhance your stay.

TIPPING GUIDELINES FOR HOTELS

The ultimate decision to tip, when to tip, and how to tip is yours. As you experiment with different situations using your own judgment, these decisions will become easier to make. However, the following will provide you with some guidelines that have served me well and are based on my own extensive experience as a cost-conscious luxury traveler.

The following is an example of how it pays to tip a little extra in the beginning in order to receive preferential treatment for the remainder of your stay. Whenever I first arrive at a hotel, I customarily tip the valet parking attendants an amount that is dependent on the regional location, usually two to three dollars. In higher priced cities such as New York, I will tip as much as four dollars when I first arrive at the hotel. Then, whenever I request my car, I will tip the attendants one to two dollars. (My average tip when I request my car is two dollars; I only tip one dollar if I am in a region with a low cost of living.) If my car has been washed or I receive some other exceptional service, I will tip three or four dollars.

As a side note, usually the only time I tip the valet when I drop off my car is when I initially arrive at a hotel or if the valet assists me with my golf clubs or some other large parcels. Other than those instances, I usually only tip the valet when they retrieve my car for me. The decision as to whether to tip when you drop off your car is a judgment call; I listen to my gut feelings based on my cumulative experiences of traveling.

If you tip the bell staff wisely and add a few extra dollars to the initial tip, they will be friendly and accommodating throughout your visit, making you feel welcomed and appreciated. When you return laden with packages from a day of shopping, they will rush to your aid, or they will quickly seek out a cab and perform any task that you might need completed. And as you can see from my friend John's story above, the bell staff can do a lot more for you than just carry your bags or call you a cab. They can also help you secure a luxurious upgraded room or access to the concierge or club levels when the front desk staff cannot. These individuals should be tipped accordingly when they provide exceptional service. Also, if you plan to revisit this hotel, make sure that on your departure you graciously thank the staff and let them know that you plan to write a letter to the hotel general manager that praises particular employees for their exceptional service. (By the way, later in this chapter I will explain when and how to tip the front desk staff for upgraded rooms and other services.)

Mark and Donna, the infrequent travelers whom we met earlier, were very successful in securing an excellent Disney World package through the successful use of tipping. Mark had traveled to Orlando in advance of Donna and their two children in order to attend a business meeting. After Mark checked into his hotel, a bellman carried his bags to his room. On their way to the room, Mark told the bellman that his wife and two children would be arriving in two days. Mark also inquired about the type of suites the hotel offered, then asked if the bellman might help to arrange a suite for him and his family. Mark told the bellman that this was his family's first trip to Walt Disney World, and he really wanted it to be special. Mark then tipped the bellman ten dollars and told him that if there was any way he could help with a suite he would "be even more appreciative." The next day, the bellman approached Mark in the lobby and told him that he was able to secure a nice suite for his family. When the bellman showed Mark the suite, Mark tipped the bellman another $50. While this might sound like a lot of money, it was well worth it, because instead of squeezing his entire family into one small room, Mark now had a spacious two-room suite with a private balcony overlooking a lush golf course. In fact, Mark's generous yet prudent manner of tipping ended up saving him money, because the bellman was so pleased with his tip that he also arranged free meal vouchers in the hotel's restaurant for Mark and his family.

It has been my experience that unlike the bell staff, front desk staff, and valet parking staff, many hotel concierges (except those located on the dedicated concierge or club floors) tend to be somewhat condescending and less likely to go out of their way for you unless they are convinced of being tipped impressively. It has also been my experience that concierges are more demanding as to the amount they expect from you, whereas I have found most of the bell staff, valet parking staff, and front desk representatives to be very appreciative of any reasonable tip. Additionally, throughout my travels I have failed in my attempts to have a concierge on the main floor or lobby upgrade me to a prime luxurious room. They can be useful in making dinner reservations, but they have also been known to send unsuspecting tourists on excursions from which the concierge has a vested interest or receives a monetary kickback. Of course this is not a hard and fast rule, and in some hotels a concierge will be a valuable ally. However, if you make a habit of finding helpful and enthusiastic members of the bell staff, valet parking staff, and front desk staff, they are much more likely to greatly enhance your travel experiences.

BE CONSISTENT YET MODERATE

Remember, when tipping you do not need to be extravagant or excessive. However, you'll want to tip a sufficient amount to make an impact, enough for the staff to remember you and insure preferential service. Typically, I will tip the valet parking attendants, bell staff, and staff members in any restaurant I plan to frequent (including the hotel restaurant or any local restaurant) more upon my initial arrival, and thereafter I usually scale back to a customary tip. However, it is important to remember to distribute your tipping throughout your entire stay. That way you show the staff that you are consistent in demonstrating your appreciation for their fine quality service, which encourages them to be consistent in providing you with that service. There is also more than just thriftiness to argue against tipping excessively. If you tip excessively, you will lose the respect of the people you tip, about which I will go into more detail later in this chapter. However, remember to be fair and most importantly, demonstrate your sincere appreciation for their efforts. Your kind words are just as valuable as a monetary gratuity. The two combined will insure a luxurious experience.

Tipping the Right Employees is Imperative

Wealthy individuals can tip whomever they encounter freely and extravagantly, but essentially they are paying excessively for the service they receive. You, on the other hand, can still travel like them while maintaining thrifty economics. Instead of tipping everyone with whom you come into contact, seek out those staff members who are eager and motivated to assist you, and who earn your money by providing you with exceptional service.

Although I mentioned above that you will usually find the bell staff, valet parking staff, and front desk representatives to be highly motivated to assist you, do not limit yourself to these individuals. For example, there will be occasions when you will find that the concierge is eager and motivated to be of service, or perhaps it might be a member of the housekeeping staff. (See chart at the end of this chapter for tipping guidelines.) You might even need to go all the way to the general manager of the property. With a general manager, however, your best tip is to let them know that you will write a complimentary letter to their corporate office.

Avoid the Ducks and Seek Out the Eagles

Wherever you go, you will always find what I like to call *Ducks and Eagles*. The ducks are those workers who go about their jobs only wishing for the clock to strike quitting time. Basically, they are the ones who just go through the motions. The eagles, on the other hand, are those whom you want to find, because they are the employees who are willing to take the extra step that makes your travel experience an extraordinary one. Eagles take pride in their jobs, readily offer their services, and provide exceptional service with a genuine desire to please you and meet your needs. They are the ones who will work to upgrade you to a prime ocean front suite and make every other aspect of your stay a pleasure. Moreover, they understand the value of service, which is why you want to find these individuals and invest your tips in them. It is not advantageous to tip ducks, because they will not provide you with decent, let alone preferential, service.

Finding the eagles will take some practice. Usually eagles will greet you very courteously and exhibit a high level of enthusiasm about their job and their surroundings. Typically they will reach for your luggage or offer other services without your request, while emanating a positive, "can do" attitude. With careful observation and practice you should be able to readily spot these individuals. Consider the story of my friend John who was staying in Phoenix. He told me that he could tell right away that this young man on the bell staff was someone who would take the initiative to meet his needs. As it turned out, John was right, and he was able to spend the day golfing and the remainder of his trip being treated like a king. John's story is also a good example of how your tips do not need to be excessive and can result in a win-win situation. John recouped his twenty-dollar tip from the discounted rate he paid for green fees, and the bell person was very satisfied with the additional income. This is the type of worker you want to seek out and reward with your tips.

Conversely, a couple of good examples of ducks come from a hotel I once visited. Initially, I was thinking of asking assistance from the bellman to access the concierge floor. However, when we walked to the elevator, this bellman saw me struggling with my luggage yet failed to offer his assistance. I decided he was definitely not the person to ask about gaining access to the concierge floor. And when I had checked out and was carrying my luggage through the doors leading outside the hotel, another bellman battled me with his bell cart for space in the doorway instead of stepping aside and allowing me to pass. Another example of duck service comes from a time when I was traveling in the Czech Republic. While checking into my Prague hotel, I innocently asked a man whom I believed to be the bellman to assist me with my luggage. This man retorted offensively that I should not ask someone who is older than I to carry my luggage.

You will find ducks and eagles in a variety of situations other than inside a hotel. When making a hotel reservation, you could encounter a duck who is unwilling to search for a competitive rate, or you might find that an airline reservationist does not put forth the effort to accommodate your needs.

The point to remember is that you want to avoid the ducks and soar with the eagles. Try to spot those who seem to be unmotivated or just going through the motions and avoid them. At the same time, be on the lookout for those who will go the extra mile for you. Treat them with respect and reward their exceptional service with good tips.

It's Better to Tip After You Receive Upgrades or Other Special Services

How you offer a tip is also key to receiving preferential service. When you are ready to offer a tip, do it in a way that ensures that you will get your desired benefit in return. I know many travelers who walk up to an employee and hand them money, without receiving any preferential treatment in return. Remember that your tips are an investment, so use them wisely. Never waltz up to the front desk representative, hand him a twenty, and then say, "Oh by the way, do you have an upgrade available?" Most representatives will be less motivated to find you one, since you have already handed them money. Likewise, some individuals might find it offensive and manipulative that you handed them money and expect something in return that they might not be able to provide.

Instead, let it be known that you desire an upgrade, and state in a subtle manner that you would be very willing to show your appreciation. I do not directly say, "If you secure me an upgrade I will give you X dollars." Rather, I let them know that I will reciprocate their goodwill with my own goodwill. I might say, "I certainly would appreciate any special accommodations, and likewise I will express my appreciation." Or I might say, "On my last visit Tom upgraded me to a suite, and I really showed him how thankful I was." Remember that you may be dealing with a hotel representative who is accustomed to working with celebrities and a well-to-do clientele. Therefore, you will need to have a degree of sophistication in securing your extra amenities. If you bluntly or crudely request special consideration you might offend the representative.

When I am seeking an upgrade or other special amenities, I *do not ever tip until I receive the goods.* If you are going to invest your money, make sure that you get some sort of return for your investment. My friend Kevin's story is a case in point. Kevin went on a vacation to Disney World with his family and some friends. While checking into the hotel, Kevin handed the front desk clerk $40 and requested an upgrade. The clerk took the money and said, "I will see what I can do," then gave him room keys. Upon arriving at the room, Kevin was disappointed to discover that his room was the same as his friends who did not waste $40 with the front desk clerk.

QUICK REVIEW

- Modest yet smart tipping can pay big dividends.
- Tip a few dollars extra in the beginning to insure future preferential service.
- Tip consistently, which means tipping when you arrive, throughout your stay, and when you leave.
- The bell staff, valet parking staff, and front desk representatives can be your best allies and are therefore the people in whom you should invest most of your tips.
- Don't waste your tips on the ducks; do invest in the eagles.
- Offer your tips in a way that ensures you will receive preferential service. Know when to tip in advance and when to tip as a reward for special services rendered.

TIPPING OUTSIDE THE HOTEL INDUSTRY

Although hotels are where you will primarily invest in monetary tips, you might also find that when dining out at your favorite restaurant it can pay to tip the maitre d' so that on your next visit you will get a table even if you don't have reservations, be seated quickly, and be offered a nice, quiet table. Again, do not walk into the restaurant and hand over money to the maitre d' without some assurance that you will get a prime table. It is probably better to tip the maitre d' on the way out (if you plan to return to the restaurant and feel that the maitre d' will still be there) to insure that next time you will be treated in a preferential manner.

Occasionally you will also receive exceptional service from an employee of a car rental agency. For example, often when I return my rental car to the airport, I ask the lot attendants if they will give me a ride back to the terminal, especially if I am pressed for time in order to make my flight. In return for this preferential service, I usually tip the lot attendant five dollars, which makes him happy and saves me the usual hassle of getting back to the terminal.

Here is a reminder about the proper way to show your appreciation for exceptional service you receive from airline employees. Although monetary tipping is not appropriate, you can still show your appreciation and insure preferential service by writing a letter to the airline that praises the employee for a job well done. As discussed in Chapter Five, when an airline receives a nicely written letter from a passenger about a particular employee, that employee receives favorable treatment from their company. Telling an airline employee in advance that you will write a letter can often aid in getting them to offer you preferential service. Just remember to follow through and write the letter! Most importantly, remember that tipping is not limited to hotel, restaurant, or car rental employees, nor is it limited to monetary compensation. Tips can be utilized in many different ways and work to your advantage in receiving preferred service.

The ABCs of Tipping

A reasonable formula for influencing the behavior of others through tips includes the following steps:

- Clearly signal what you would like. Express your wishes diplomatically in terms of what you would prefer to have, rather than what you demand to have.
- Do not expect perfect compliance with your wishes. Accept the fact that you might have to accept approximations of what you want. For example, you might not get upgraded to the actual concierge floor room. Instead, you might be provided an access key to the floor. Or perhaps you might be given a suite with a nice view of the ocean rather than an oceanfront room that is not a suite.
- Recognize and reward this accommodating behavior with adequate tips and expressions of gratitude.
- Be willing to reciprocate other's goodwill with your own. Your own goodwill could take the form of monetary tips, letters, or telling a supervisor how valuable that employee is to customer service.
- Skillful use of this formula will significantly improve your ability to influence but not manipulate travel employees to positively enhance your travel experiences.

A Last Quick Caveat about Tipping

Bear in mind that you want your tips to be perceived as a genuine show of appreciation for an employee's fine service. Therefore, it is imperative that you do not come across as manipulative, arrogant, or a show-off. Maintain decorum in the way you tip and invest your tips with the same care you afford to your other financial assets. If you freely hand over tips without expressing heartfelt appreciation or without reason, you will lose respect or be seen as trying to exploit an employee. Therefore it is eminently important that tipping be closely related to a specific service you desire and receive.

Guidelines For Smart Tipping

Ground Transportation and Baggage

- Car-rental shuttle driver: none to $1 per use
- Car-rental attendant for priority return service to airport: $5–$10
- Hotel courtesy shuttle: $1; If driver helps with luggage: $2
- Taxi dispatcher: None
- Taxi driver: 10–15%
- Car service: Gratuity included, or 15% of bill
- Airport curbside baggage handler: $1–$1.50 per bag

Hotel

Remember to add a few extra dollars the first time you tip a helpful staff member for customary services.

- Parking valet: $1–$2 per use
- Front Desk: $5–$20 for a room upgrade, after you have seen the upgraded room

- Bellhop:
  —for taking luggage to room and delivering messages or packages: $1–$2 per bag or message
  —for securing a room upgrade (tip after you are escorted to the upgraded room): $5–$20

- Front Desk or Bellhop: depending on the quality of the upgrade and length of stay, up to $100 could be appropriate (use discretion)

- Front Desk or Bellhop: for access key to concierge or club floor: $5–$20

  NOTE: It is a good idea to put tips for front desk staff in an envelope with their name on it and hand the envelope to them.

- Doorman: $1–$2 for cabs and assisting with bags

- Doorman for special services: $1–$2 per day

- Manager of hotel: Write a letter

- Housekeeper: $1–$2 per day; for special services (cleaning at special times, special treats in the room): $2–$5 per day

- Room Service: 15–20%; if service is included in bill: 5% or $1 minimum

- Message service: $1–$2 per delivery

- Concierge for theater tickets or making special accommodations: $5–$10

- Upon departure: let the most helpful employees know that you plan to write a complimentary letter to the hotel's general manager.

RESTAURANT

- Maitre d': for a good table: $5 for two persons: $10 for four or more (double the amount for five-star restaurants)
- Waiters: 15–20% of bill; if gratuities are included, an additional amount is warranted for special services.
- Bartender: 15% of liquor bill
- Wine steward: 10% of wine bill

AIRLINE EMPLOYEES

- Write a letter

OTHER

- Rail porter: $1 per bag
- Hat/coat check: $1 per coat or per person

NOTE: There are different tipping customs in different regions, particularly in different countries. For example, in Europe your tips may be included in your bill (in restaurants and even in hotels), and therefore you have to be careful not to over tip. Be sure to consult a regional guidebook for specific guidelines.

10

Buyer Beware

Sound Advice For the Penny Pinching Luxury Traveler

Whenever I wish to see a countryside or historic ruins, I avoid group tours, which are not my style of travel. I learned this when I took a bus tour that claimed to be a means of visiting notable sights in Thailand. The trip began with numerous stops at hotels to take on a busload of tourists making for a crowded and uncomfortable ride. Then I discovered that the cumulative time spent sightseeing was minute in comparison to the time spent at a tourist trap shopping mall that charged prices marked up in excess of 200%. In frustration, I left and took a taxi back to my hotel. On subsequent occasions, I have avoided such disasters by finding reputable local guides who give me firsthand knowledge of the region. This has not only allowed me to avoid tourist traps, typically it also costs only a fraction of what a tour operator would charge.

There are many ways to avoid misleading offers like the "tour" I took in Thailand, save money, and enjoy a totally first class experience in the process. In this chapter we will focus on the most efficient means of touring unfamiliar regional areas and how to protect yourself financially and personally, particularly while traveling to foreign countries.

If You're Looking for Bargains, Avoid Tourist Traps

I discovered in Thailand the disadvantages of being lured into a supposedly "great tour," only to find out that it was nothing more than a pricey and dishonorable means of getting me to a designated emporium designed to sell me overpriced goods. This story raises some important considerations for the penny pinching luxury traveler, beginning with the obvious notation that while traveling, you will find no shortage of ways to spend your money. This is certainly true if you are on vacation. There will always be enticing souvenirs to buy, tours to take, events to attend. Although many of these experiences are what makes traveling fun, you will want to minimize frivolous spending. Therefore, think twice about what you are about to spend your money on. It is usually best to step back from the emotional excitement of the moment and use your best judgment.

For example, many tourists in Hawai'i visit galleries and fall in love with a piece of art. Most often that piece of art is overpriced and can be purchased on the mainland for considerably less money. That is not to say that all art in Hawai'i is an imprudent purchase. I have purchased art while traveling in Hawai'i. What I suggest, however, is to stay away from the main tourist locales when shopping for art or other regional specialty items. Seek advice from a unbiased employee at your hotel, someone like the manager or perhaps someone who works in the restaurant where you are having a meal. In other words, try to seek the advice of someone who has been there for a while and *does not have a vested interest in how you spend your money.*

When you are shopping for art, try to find out how long the gallery has been in business, what artists they work with, and if they have other locations. The artists they represent will give you an idea of how established the gallery is. If they only work with one artist, they may be limited in their scope. If they have multiple locations, this will indicate some stability. A single location might indicate that they are small or might not have been in business long. If you're serious, find a gallery that is well-established; it is more likely to want to build a long term relationship with its customers and would be less likely to give you a bad deal.

Do not succumb to the pressure of a gallery owner telling you that if you do not buy a piece now, it will be sold. Instead, tell the gallery that you are interested in the piece but would like to think it over, and request that it be placed on hold. Sometimes the gallery might require a small deposit. If that is the case, make sure that your deposit is refundable, get a receipt that says so in writing, and put your deposit on a credit card. Placing the piece on hold gives you an opportunity to determine if this is something you really want and if you even have room for it in your home. On a number of occasions, my wife and I thought that we absolutely needed a piece of art, only to discuss it more thoroughly over dinner and realize that it would not even work in our home.

SIGHTSEEING IN STYLE AND SAFETY

Another easy way to spend money is by taking a tour. Many tour operators in vacation destinations offer reputable tours, unlike the particular tour I took in Thailand. One of the best ways to determine which tours will offer you a peak experience is to consult a regional guidebook. Guidebooks are also an excellent way to discover restaurants and unique shops or galleries. You can also find out about reputable tours by asking the hotel manager, front desk representatives, bell staff, or even the hotel's restaurant staff. As I mentioned earlier in the book, you can also consult the hotel's concierge; however, be aware that while many concierges will have your best interests in mind, some might be influenced by the percentage they sometimes earn by recommending a specific tour.

If you would rather not take organized group tours and desire something more private and comfortable, consider hiring a local guide. I have been successful in seeking out knowledgeable guides who have taken me exactly where I wished to travel and saved me the inconvenience of riding in a large, diesel-emitting bus that stops every five minutes to pick up new passengers. However, you must be extremely careful about whom you select as a guide. In some cities it is not uncommon for tourists to be kidnapped or driven to a remote location and stripped of all their worldly goods. In Mexico City, for instance, there have been numerous cases of tourists being assaulted and robbed by taxi drivers. The taxis to avoid are usually those cruising the streets. In fact, in Mexico City you should never hail a cab on the street, but should accept rides only in taxis you have ordered by phone or obtained through a hotel.

But don't be paranoid; a trustworthy taxi driver or other local guide can significantly enhance your travels. My friend Lance found such a driver who took him on a shopping trip in Indonesia. Lance felt comfortable enough with this driver to leave his shopping bags in the taxi while he continued shopping. A few of my pleasurable journeys that were led by private local guides have been treks through Jamaica and the English countryside. To insure my safety, I usually ask my hotel for referrals to reputable and trustworthy private guides, or I hire an off-duty hotel employee. I have found that the price is usually more reasonable than an organized group tour and always of higher quality, since private local guides will usually know the hidden secrets of your destination. When you combine this approach with the knowledge you will gain from regional guidebooks, you will have a unique travel experience that few mass tours can rival.

ADDITIONAL TIPS ON TAXIS

If you don't have a rental car, taking taxis can be a good alternative to mass public transportation. However, when using taxicabs keep in mind the following: most cities require that private drivers, taxicabs, and motor coaches or buses must have a city permit to operate. Therefore, make sure that you use a driver, taxicab, or bus that is licensed by the city to perform these services. If there is a meter in the cab, insist that it be used. If there is a plaque in the cab explaining various surcharges, read it.

If you are at the airport or train station, go to the designated taxi stand and use a taxi only from that designated stand. If you have a question about transportation services, you should find a booth at the airport or the train station marked "Information." Inquire with them about the accredited modes of transportation. If you need to take a taxi from your hotel, only use the ones that are waiting in front of your hotel and will be waved forward by the hotel's door attendant. Within many cities you will find designated taxi areas; use these areas to insure that you get into a safe taxi. If you are dining out and are not in an area where there is a taxi stand, ask your waiter to call you a taxi. By the time you have finished with your coffee and dessert, the taxi will be waiting there ready to whisk you safely away. When you are at a museum or area where large crowds gather, be sure that you go to the taxi stand or look for a taxi that has the appropriate credentials.

If the taxi does not have a meter, be sure to discuss what the rate should be in advance. Some of the unlicensed taxis will charge unsuspecting tourists unfair rates, as I discovered first-hand. Once while traveling from the airport in Madrid to my hotel, I paid an unlicensed taxi $85. While checking into the hotel I saw a couple who were on my flight and asked them how they got to the hotel. They said they took a taxi, and it only cost them $25.

CREDIT CARDS AND DEBIT CARDS

While traveling you will have a variety of options for handling the money you've set aside for your trip. Although travelers' checks are still a popular alternative to cash, I recommend credit cards as the best choice for cost-conscious travelers. Credit cards offer several clear advantages: you can dispute erroneous charges, obtain favorable exchange rates, and avoid carrying large amounts of cash. Furthermore, credit cards are easy to use, you can replace them if lost or stolen, you can also earn points in you frequent flyer accounts by using certain cards.

My good friend Rich and his wife recently traveled to Europe for the first time. After their return, Rich told me how amazed he was to be able to turn a corner and get money from a local ATM when he ran out of cash. What Rich discovered is a simple fact that has made traveling easier for millions of people. By accessing local ATMs with your credit card, debit card, or your bank ATM card, you are afforded the security of only having to carry small amounts of cash on you. When traveling overseas, you get the bank's exchange rate, which is the most favorable rate anyone can get. And if you are traveling from country to country you can take out only what you need and avoid returning home with a bunch of unused foreign currency. Moreover, credit cards can be used virtually anywhere throughout the world.

Paying for your travels with a credit card provides one advantage that neither cash nor travelers' checks can match. That is, if you have difficulties with your purchase, be it a hotel, car rental, piece of art, tour, or anything you charge on your card, you can dispute the charge with the credit card company. I paid for the tour I took in Thailand with my American Express card. When I returned home I called American Express and told them that I felt I was cheated and wanted to dispute the charge. Immediately, the representative reversed the charges and initiated an investigation. As you will see later in this chapter, there are many travel scams, and using a credit card can help you to recoup your losses.

Many of the premium credit cards, such as gold and platinum cards, offer enhanced travel amenities and travel protection. Your credit card might provide you with upgrade opportunities if you use their card to pay for the hotel or even an airline ticket. Some cards will cover insurance on rental cars, provide flight insurance in case of an accident, offer lost baggage insurance, or guarantee a rain-check for the trip in case of cancellation (usually this is for a cruise or a resort that gets rained out). Some cards also provide specialized overseas travel emergency assistance, such as transporting you to a hospital that maintains the same high standards as American hospitals or providing legal assistance, if needed. Your premium credit cards can also provide you with emergency cash if you find yourself stranded, and the companies will replace a lost or stolen card in 24 hours or less.

As an alternative to a credit card, I like to use my bank's debit card, which works like a Visa, but instead of using credit, the money is pulled right out of my bank account.

A Last Word on Safety

Consult regional guidebooks and web sites for travel safety information, especially the travel warning web site for the U.S. Department of State at http://travel.state.gov/travel_warnings.html. Another good source is World Travel Watch at http://www.travelerstales.com/wtw/wtw.html. A good guidebook or web site will warn you about the potential dangers of particular regional areas and how to avoid putting yourself at risk. It pays to know in advance about what precautions to take.

Sounds Too Good to Be True? It Probably Is

"World-class offer for a free Bahamas vacation."

"Two Weeks in Hawaii for $350!"

"You Have Won a Free Vacation, Call 1 900 555-5555 to Claim."

"You Have Just Won Complimentary Hotel Lodgings to an Exotic Location."

"Buy This Right Now and Get Free Airfare to a Vacation Resort."

Have you been approached with any of these fantastic travel bargains? Each year in this country, over 12 billion dollars is lost to travel fraud and scams.

There are many ways the unsuspecting traveler can fall prey to mail or telephone solicitations for free or discounted vacation "deals" that not only seem too good to be true, they are.

When researching travel opportunities, you will come across many tempting offers. Unfortunately, many of them may be fraudulent. Nationally, travel fraud is one of the top ten scams in the United States, with the U.S. Postal Inspection Service identifying bogus vacation offers as one of the top five. *The Wall Street Journal* reported on one air carrier that advertised an extremely low (and nonexistent) fare on a flight. In fact, the flight itself did not exist.

Typical scam operators start with a postcard, certificate, or phone call stating that you have been selected to receive a free vacation—after you pay a "one-time membership fee" or "handling charge." Sometimes you might be told about a wonderful vacation destination, except that you will not be given any details about your trip until you pay some sort of fee. And then when you hear those details, they either involve other hidden costs or the vacation itself bears little resemblance to what you were promised. Another popular scam is to send out a postcard that will instruct you, the recipient, to call a 900-number in order to claim your prize. While on the line you discover (at the end of a lengthy sales pitch) that you will have to pay some sort of fee to claim that prize, and in the meantime the clock is ticking away on the phone charges, as you are being charged by the 900 service for every minute you are on the line. Some victims of the 900 scam have paid over one hundred dollars in phone charges.

It is relatively easy for con artists to scam the public, because so many people want to take a vacation, and understandably get excited about a supposedly great deal. However, when you arrive at your destination (if you ever do arrive), it becomes apparent why the price was so low, and quickly your enthusiasm turns to displeasure. A fraudulent brochure might show ocean front accommodations, but when you get there you might find that there are no such rooms in the hotel. Or the hotel will be run down, old, and ugly; definitely nothing like what you were promised.

SMART WAYS TO AVOID TRAVEL FRAUD

The best way to avoid falling prey to travel frauds and scams is to adhere to the principles I have emphasized throughout this book: restrict your business to well-established, high quality travel companies, and take control of and responsibility for your own travel planning. Become a student of the travel industry. Today's travelers have at their disposal 800-numbers, the Internet, and specialized travel planning software that can easily assist them in researching travel destinations with reputable companies. When you research your travel destinations, you will know in advance what kind of value you will be receiving for your money. I cannot count how many travelers have told me crushing stories of disappointment upon arriving at a travel destination, when prior to their arrival they were excited about what they were going to get and how much money they were going to save.

As I have emphasized throughout this book, the key principle to receiving low-cost, luxury travel is by virtue of your history as a loyal, paying customer whose repeat business is the incentive for quality companies to reciprocate with preferential treatment. In this arrangement, you and the company benefit mutually. That is why you need to ask yourself when faced with an unbelievable bargain from an unknown company if there is the possibility for the company as well as for you to benefit. If it doesn't seem possible, then it may very well be a fraudulent offer that will only serve to part you from your money and give you little more than aggravation and disappointment in return.

If you find yourself tempted nonetheless, be alert for the following signs of travel fraud. If a travel company or salesperson exhibits any of these signs, don't even think about spending your money with them.

- High pressure to buy now or make a large deposit—or else the offer will be gone
- Promises of a deal that seems too good to be true
- Inappropriate request for credit card or other personal information
- 900-numbers
- Restrictions against using the travel voucher for sixty days (the deadline for disputing a credit card charge)
- Agencies or companies that use P.O. boxes as an address, have toll free numbers that go unanswered, or refuse to take credit cards
- If you have access to the Internet, search the worldwide web for reports of travel frauds and scams and make note of these companies and offers as ones to avoid. To conduct your search, type in "travel fraud" or "travel scams" on your Internet search engine.

INSTANT TRAVEL AGENT

Another twist on travel scams are untrained travel agents offering travel services. Many people do not realize that it is possible for someone to become a travel agent simply by paying a fee. There are companies that offer individuals "instant" travel agent credentials in return for this fee and their agreement to solicit friends to join the program as well. Moreover, many of these companies pressure these new travel agents to sell trips to locations where the company has bought bulk certificates. These vouchers are cheap to the company because they are laden with restrictions that are passed on to you. These restrictions can include limiting travel to certain time periods, requiring you to make reservations a certain time in advance, mandating that your stay be a certain number of days, or requiring that your stay include certain days such as Saturday night. With these vouchers it is possible that you will have a vacation, but it is seldom what you were led to expect.

Selecting a Reputable Travel Agent or Other Travel Company

This brings up another point. If you do use a travel agent to help you design a vacation, try to go to one who is well-traveled and highly experienced as a travel agent. If your agent has only read travel brochures, he or she will probably not be able to offer you a lot of firsthand knowledge. In these cases, you would probably do just as well to make your own travel arrangements and buy a reputable travel guidebook. Finally, buying airline tickets from an unknown individual opens yourself up to purchasing stolen tickets. If this happens to you, the ticket will be confiscated and you could possibly face criminal charges, and at the very least be questioned by authorities.

Here are some helpful guidelines for selecting reputable travel agents or travel companies:

- Check with the Better Business Bureau to see if there have been any complaints or pending legal action against the travel agent or company.

- Ask the agency or company how long they have been in business and ask the agents what their personal travel experience is.
- Only use travel agents who are certified with the American Society of Travel Agents (ASTA).

COUPON BROKERS: A RISKY VENTURE

On occasion, I have spoken with individuals who have purchased airline tickets through coupon brokers. Most often the traveler ended up getting burned. First of all, by purchasing your tickets through coupon brokers, you will not get any frequent flyer miles or continue to build loyalty with an airline. In addition, when buying tickets from coupon brokers you do not get to confirm your seats. Therefore, you might arrive at the airport and find that your reservation is not in the airline's reservation system. And in some cases, you may end up paying for a ticket you never receive.

Selling your miles to a coupon broker is also a bad idea. These brokers sometimes operate under shady circumstances and most definitely without any authority from the airlines. Under present law these coupon brokers do not violate any federal or state laws; however, they most certainly infringe upon stipulations made in the printed information of the airlines' frequent flyer programs. If the airlines find out that you sold a free ticket you earned to a coupon broker, they will deny boarding on the ticket and most likely close your frequent flyer account. These harsh penalties are just not worth it. Instead, use your extra miles to give free tickets and upgrades to family and friends.

Also, as mentioned above, there are some reports that coupon brokers have pulled fast ones on both ticket sellers and buyers. Under this scam they promise to sell your miles to a buyer, then collect those miles from you in the form of a ticket, but disappear before paying you. Or they will offer to sell you a ticket, insist you pay for the ticket in advance, and disappear with your money. Moreover some coupon brokers could use the information they gained from you about your frequent flyer account (such as account numbers or PIN codes) to pilfer miles from your account. My advice is to stick to the straight and narrow, avoid the gimmicks, and focus on luxurious travels.

TIMESHARES

Although I do not mean to imply that the selling of timeshare vacations is by nature a fraudulent practice, and while admittedly my knowledge of timeshares is limited, you should be aware of their potential disadvantages. After buying a timeshare, many people have felt that they were misled about what a good investment it was and how it would enable them to travel to many different locations. The usual complaints were an inability to trade for other locations or an inability to sell the timeshare for the same amount of money they paid, let alone make a profit. Other buyers have found that the buildings and grounds of the timeshare property were not always maintained properly over time. If you are looking for a guaranteed place to stay in a particular location for a particular week or weeks during the year, then a timeshare might be what you want. But if you're looking for flexibility of destinations and a return on your investment, make sure you do a lot of research before you buy.

Another very common complaint about timeshares is that the people who sell them can be very aggressive. Commonly you will have to sit through an interminably long sales presentation, then be pushed into making a decision on the spot. To entice you to attend the sales presentation you will be offered free boat rides, dinners, electronic equipment, or a free stay at a hotel, whatever the promoters think is an enticing lure. However, you might find that the length and pressure of the sales presentation outweighs any free incentives you might be offered.

You should also be wary of timeshare sales companies that are located offshore, because they would not be subject to many of the U.S. consumer protection laws. On the other hand, there are some very well established companies who offer timeshare properties, including The Marriott Hotels, The Hilton Hotel Corporation, and The Walt Disney Company. If you find timeshare traveling appealing, you should consider contacting one of these or other reputable companies.

PROMOTION SCAMS

One last "deal" to watch for is the promotion scam. This would involve a company that says if you buy their product (such as a car, television, washer/dryer, or other item), they will give you free airfare to a fabulous resort or a certain number of days at a resort hotel. This is a particularly enticing scam, because often the companies who offer the airfare or hotel stays are very reputable and trusted companies. The problem is that the company from whom you bought the product gives you a certificate or some form of a voucher for your travel and that's it. When you read the fine print on these vouchers, you discover that you need to fly on a designated airline paying a specific fare basis in order to get your free hotel room, or you need to stay at a hotel and pay a mandatory rate in order to get your free airfare. These rates are often higher than you might find on your own. The key here is to look at the real cost involved and read the fine print before you make any commitments.

Maintain Your Own Integrity

You, the traveler, also have a responsibility to act in an ethical manner. For example, I have read numerous articles and books advocating enticing airfare trickery that breaks airline rules and at the very least is questionable and shady. Although you may profit in the short run from some of these tricks—which I will not mention in this book—the possible consequences include: having your tickets confiscated or voided, being denied boarding, or losing your frequent flyer account. Above all, you are building a long-term relationship with your travel partners, and as with any partners, you do not want to deceive them. I have flown over 500 flights in first class paying coach fares and have never cheated the system.

Bona Fide Deals

Just as you should be wary of travel frauds and deals that are too good to be true, you should always be on the lookout for legitimate discounts and travel deals.

Some advantageous and legitimate discounts:

- Senior citizen airline discounts or books of discount airline coupons that can be bought at discounted rates. These rates and discounts are offered by most of the major air carriers.
- Likewise, many airlines offer similar discounts to students.
- Airfare Wars. The best deals to profit from are the airfare

wars, which have been a common occurrence over the past few years.

- Book Early. You can often get the best rates if you can book your travel early and do your homework while maintaining flexibility.
- Companion Fares. In many cases, you can buy one ticket and get a companion ticket for free or half price.
- The AAA Discount. This very reputable automobile club offers its members a wide range of discounts from airlines to hotels, to cruise ships and rental cars. In addition, they have a resourceful travel staff to assist members with their travel plans.
- Last minute fares. Many airlines and hotels have "last minute fares" when they have not been able to book the desired number of passengers or guests for a particular flight or day. These last minute specials, which are distributed via e-mail, are a great way to save if you are flexible and can travel without much notice. To get on these e-mail lists, contact your travel partner.

As often is the case in life, there are no real shortcuts. Take the time to become a prudent consumer of reputable travel companies' services and you'll experience the peace of mind that comes with first class travel.

Key Points

➢ ***Think twice before you spend.***
If you are considering buying a costly piece of art, sleep on it. If you are considering taking an organized tour, be sure it will not lead to a tourist trap.

➢ *Exercise caution whenever you consider hiring a private guide.*
The right guide can be a wonderful alternative to organized group tours. The wrong one can be dangerous. Consider hiring an off-duty hotel employee or someone recommended by your hotel.

➢ *Take only licensed cabs or buses.*
Go to designated taxi stands, or have the hotel or restaurant call you a cab.

➢ *Credit cards offer the best protection for your money, no matter where you travel.*

➢ *Look for signs of travel fraud.*
Avoid deals that involve high pressure, 900-numbers, inappropriate requests for credit card numbers, or a 60-day waiting period to use a purchased travel voucher.

➢ *Be wary.*
Steer clear of companies that have P.O. boxes as an address, toll free numbers that go unanswered, or refuse to take credit cards. Search the worldwide web for travel scams.

➢ *Check your travel company's references.*
Stick to well-established travel companies and travel agents who are affiliated with ASTA. Ask the Better Business Bureau about them.

➢ *Avoid coupon brokers.*
You could end up losing miles, money, or even your frequent flyer account, without getting anything in return.

➢ *Watch out for promotion scams.*
The travel vouchers you receive in return for purchasing

merchandise are often laden with restrictions that involve costly hotel rates and airfares.

- ***Look carefully at timeshare offers.***
  These offers often sound better than they are. Although there are certainly some reputable timeshare companies, be sure of what you're getting before you make a commitment.

And Now You're on Your Way

The Greek word *apeiros*, which means unbounded or endless, aptly describes the travel experience ahead of you. I hope this book has laid down a simple foundation and will help you make the most of your travels. Whether your journeys lead you to ancient ruins, a pristine beach, or on a typical business trip, you can be confident in the knowledge that you are treating yourself to a memorable experience. For while the aim of this book is to enhance your travels, the underlying message is a reminder to tend to your soul.

We all need to take time for ourselves away from the constraints of our daily life, our job, our family responsibilities, and our social or civic duties to relax, recuperate, or seek our own spiritual rejuvenation. My own travels have taught me the humble nature of our lives and inspired me with awe.

My first experience of transcending my everyday reality and entering into another world was on my first overseas trip to Rome. I sat in the Coliseum stunned by the magnificence of this two thousand-year-old edifice as my mind was transported back to the time of its origin. I thought how amazing it was that a society, which by today's standards possessed limited resources and technology, could construct such a wonderful monument for future generations unforeseen by its creators.

Carrying on with my journey through Italy, I ventured into the magnificent rooms of the Vatican, where I was surrounded by art known throughout the world. Finally I was experiencing the masterpieces of Michelangelo firsthand. These priceless beauties changed my perspective on life, and gave me a whole new passion for experiencing the manifold treasures of our world.

It is my hope that this book will open up a whole new dimension to the way you travel, one in which you discover the beauties of this Earth while treating yourself and your family to relaxation and luxury .

My best to you, and may your journeys fulfill your innermost desires.

Resources And References

Books, Magazines, Newspapers, Radio

To assist in your research, I have compiled the following list of travel resources. You will also want to consult your local newspaper, in-flight magazines, and regional guidebooks.

BOOKS

Arrive in Better Shape: How to Avoid Jet Lag and Travel Stress
By Farrol Kahn (New York: Harper Prism, 1996)
With hints, tips, and suggestions from veteran airline personnel and other frequent flyers, this book can help make take-offs and landings much easier. You will discover the ideal way to prepare for a long trip, how to readjust yourself on landing, and even what to take to make the flight comfortable and relaxing for you.

Consumer Reports 1999 Best Travel Deals
By Ed Perkins with Walt Leonard (New York: Consumer Reports, 1999)
This is the quintessential guide edited by the authors of the of *Consumer Reports Travel Letter* offering an encyclopedic base of information on all aspects of the travel industry. Each year this book is revised with the most up-to-date toll free numbers, web sites, and other relevant information of travel operators.

Tips for the Savvy Traveler
By Deborah Burns, Suzanne Tore (Pownal,VT: Storey Books, 1997)
Offers sound advice on health, security, customs, packing, jet lag, the travel industry, and more. This book enables a traveler to minimize frustration and maximize enjoyment and discovery.

Travelers' Tales

This publisher offers an excellent series of travel books, including destination-oriented anthologies (*America, San Francisco, Italy, Paris, Thailand* and more), special edition travel anthologies (*The Road Within, Women in the Wild, A Woman's World, Food,* among others), and books on strategies for travel (such as *Safety and Security for Women Who Travel, Gutsy Women: Travel Tips and Wisdom for the Road*).

EDITORIAL ADDRESS:

Travelers' Tales
P.O. Box 610160
Redwood City CA 94061 USA

PHONE ORDERS: 800 998-9938

WEB SITE: www.travelerstales.com

EMAIL: ttales@travelerstales.com

Travel Rights

By Charles Leocha (Hampstead, OH: World Leisure, 1998)

A handy, compact book by travel authority Charles Leocha that's stocked with basic, essential advice for frequent travelers. Topics include: advice on dealing with airlines, travel agents, car rental companies; dealing with lost or damaged baggage; benefits available through credit card usage; how to avoid sales tax; plus suggestions on how to make complaints that get action. Available in bookstores and by mail.

PRICE: $7.95; $11.70 includes shipping and handling

MAIL ORDERS:

Book World Services
P.O. Box 18088
Sarasota, FL 34276

PHONE ORDERS: 800 444-2524

The Unofficial Business Traveler's Pocket Guide: 165 Tips Even the Best Business Traveler May Not Know
By Christopher J. McGinnis (New York: McGraw-Hill, 1998)
This book includes information on surviving the airport, surviving the plane, eating right, staying healthy and managing stress. This is a good source of information for both the seasoned veteran as well as the first time flyer.

Wendy Perrin's Secrets Every Smart Traveler Should Know
By Wendy Perrin (New York: Fodor's Travel Publications, 1996)
Edited by the consumer travel expert of the *Condé Nast Traveler* magazine, this book offers an inside perspective and advice that will assist travelers of all levels. An excellent resource to add to your library.

Bookstores Online
Online bookstores are valuable resources for travel books and guides of all kinds, as well as reviews and reader commentary. Many independent bookstores have a good online presence, such as Book Passage, Powell's, The Tattered Cover, Travellers Bookstore. Chains such as Borders and Barnes & Noble have good sites, and Amazon.com is a useful reference. But don't forget your local bookstore, which is often the best place to find travel books and magazines.

Magazines and Newsletters

Condé Nast Traveler
This is the one magazine I make sure to read as soon as I receive it. I have found this publication to offer excellent tips and well researched, full-length articles covering off-season, general, and exotic travel. Readers will also find insightful tips in regu-

lar features like the Perrin Report and Travel Ombudsman.

U.S. SUBSCRIPTION RATE: $15 a year

MAIL ORDERS:

Condé Nast Traveler
P.O. Box 57018
Boulder, CO 80322-7018

PHONE ORDERS: 800 777-0700

Consumer Reports Travel Letter

This consumer-oriented 12-page monthly newsletter features no advertising and short, information-packed articles that can save you money and help avoid rip-offs. It focuses on insider's tips, business information, and travel health news with know-your-rights articles and quality test reports. Each edition has a reference index that covers subjects from the last 12 issues referenced by topic, month, and page number.

U.S. SUBSCRIPTION RATES: $39 per year; $59 for two years

MAIL ORDERS:

Subscription Director
Consumer Reports Travel Letter
P.O. Box 53629
Boulder, CO 80322-3629 USA

PHONE ORDERS: 800 234-1970

Frequent Flyer

Published "for business people, who must travel," by the Official Airlines Guide. Full color at approximately 100 pages, this monthly magazine serves as an excellent resource for the frequent traveler. Most articles run less than two pages, are easy to read, and packed with information on a wide range of topics of interest to the frequent traveler.

U.S. SUBSCRIPTION RATE: $24 a year, magazine only. With

subscription to OAG Pocket Flight Guide: $86 a year
PHONE ORDERS: 800 323-3537, ext. 1065

InsideFlyer

Edited by Randy Petersen, who is considered by many travelers and mileage junkies as the guru of Miles Programs. This exclusive magazine offers a focus on frequent travel plans covering airlines, hotels, car rental companies, and credit cards. This monthly publication offers a reliable resource for travelers who want to maximize their frequent mile programs. Additionally, travelers will find the most timely information on how to get bonus points and upgrade opportunities. Contact them for a sample copy.

U.S. SUBSCRIPTION RATE: $36 a year
MAIL ORDERS:
Subscription Department
InsideFlyer
4715-C Town Center Drive
Colorado Springs, CO 80916-4709
PHONE ORDERS: 800 209-2870
FAX ORDERS: 719 597-6855

InsideFlyer—International Edition

A new source of information for frequent flyers who reside outside the Americas. It highlights award and bonus programs from Europe, Asia, Africa, and the South Pacific. International frequent flyers will have access to the same sought-after information U.S. frequent travelers have come to rely upon in a 16-to-20-page monthly magazine format.

SUBSCRIPTION RATE: UK residents—£30 for one year; Europe residents—£45 for one year; residents outside Europe—£50 for one year.

MAIL ORDERS:
Frequent Flyer Services
InsideFlyer International Edition
24-8 The Coda Centre
189 Munster Road
London SW6 6AW UK
PHONE ORDERS: 01-71-385-6412
FAX ORDERS: 01-71-386-9421

InsideFlyer Miles & Money:
A Personal Finance Guide for Frequent Flyers
A three part series exploring mileage-earning opportunities from purchasing or leasing cars, stock trading, shopping, investing, and more ways to earn frequent flyer miles than you ever thought of. (This article appeared on the insideflyer web, and offers excellent information on how to gain ancillary miles.) Contact InsideFlyer magazine or their website.
WEB SITE: www.webflyer.com

National Geographic Traveler
Published bimonthly by the well-respected National Geographic Society, *National Geographic Traveler* is a magazine with an exclusive focus on travel. Readers can find help for all aspects of their travel plans, from detailed maps to lodging recommendations.
U.S. SUBSCRIPTION RATE: $17.99 per year; $29.99 for two years
MAIL ORDERS:
National Geographic Traveler
P.O. Box 63002
Tampa, Florida 33663-3002
PHONE ORDERS: 800 NGS-LINE (800 647-5463)

Travel & Leisure

A lifesyle magazine that explores vacation and business travel destinations, leisure-time pursuits, hotels, restaurants, and entertainment. Departments and features present a blend of travel and value.

U.S. SUBSCRIPTION RATE: $39 a year

PHONE ORDERS: 800 888-8728

NEWSPAPERS

USA Today

Every Tuesday, *USA Today's* Money section runs a business travel column featuring trends affecting frequent travelers. Here you'll find the latest news in fares, promotions, and award programs together with hot tips for road warriors such as the latest travel gadgets and accessories, and which airports offer lounge areas for smokers.

U.S. SUBSCRIPTION RATE: $156 a year; corresponding rates for under 52 weeks also available

PHONE ORDERS: 800 USA-0001

Wall Street Journal

Friday's edition includes a travel section that is useful for staying current on travel trends, average travel costs, and provides insightful travel tips.

SUBSCRIPTION RATE: 26 weeks for $89, 52 weeks $175

Wall Street Interactive Edition: www.wsj.com ($29 per year for print subscribers, $59 per year for non-subscribers)

SUBSCRIBER SERVICES: 800 909-8899

Radio

The Savvy Traveler
Each week on National Public Radio, Rudy Maxa offers a diverse list of guests with colorful stories, insightful tips, and practical recommendations designed to make travel easier and fun. (Saturdays, 5–6 p.m. PST. Programming times may differ in your local area.)

Internet Research Tools for Airfares, Flight Availability, Hotels

United Connection
Software by United Airlines that allows you to reserve and purchase travel with over 500 airlines, 30,000 hotels, and 45 car rental companies. If you fly with United Airlines you can receive bonus miles and upgrade your air ticket at the time of making your reservation.
WEB SITE DOWNLOAD: www.ual.com
PHONE ORDER: 800 4UA-CNXN

Small Luxury Hotels
Provides a detailed listing of some of the finest quality hotels around the globe. Consider sampling the sophistication of The Ritz in London, the elegance of Raffles Hotel in Singapore, and the glamour and charm of resort hotels, historic châteaux, and country houses throughout the world. The Small Luxury Hotels stamp guarantees an unequalled level of privacy, luxury, and exclusivity. Their web site offers the ease of booking and familiarity of an international hotel chain through its automated reservation system while at the same time retaining and

promoting the unique character and independence of each of its members.

NORTH AMERICAN OFFICE
1716 Banks Street
Houston, Texas, 77098
PHONE: 713 522-9512
FAX: 713 524-7412
DIRECTORY REQUEST: 713 522-3159
WEB SITE: www.slh.com

The Leading Hotels of the World

This is a luxury collection of over 300 hotels located in 68 countries worldwide. Their directory provides an excellent source of luxury hotels throughout the world. Their web site offers real-time, on-line reservation capabilities. You can check room availability, rates, and make a reservation for any member hotel from their individual pages. You can sign up for a free membership and receive annual directories by contacting the corporate headquarters. (I have found that it is usually better to contact the hotels directly to receive the best rate.)

CORPORATE HEADQUARTERS
99 Park Avenue
New York, NY 10016-1601
TELEPHONE: 212 515-5600
FAX: 212 515-5898
WEB SITE: www.lhw.com

Web Sites

Below are some of my favorite Internet sites that should prove to be extremely helpful in researching excellent travel opportunities throughout the world. The list is a brief sample of available sites on the World Wide Web. To find additional sites, try the following key words with your search engine: travel, traveling, frequent flyers, airlines, airfares, and hotels.

GENERAL TRAVEL INFORMATION

This will serve as a good starting point for researching your travel planning.

America Online's travel channel—Keyword: Travel

Corporate Rate Hotel Directory—www.idt.net/corp_hotels
An interesting site where you can look up the corporate rate of a hotel before making a reservation.

Epicurious—www.epicurious.com
Site offered by *Condé Nast Traveler* with an extensive database of worldwide travel destinations.

Expedia—www.expedia.com
Site for booking airlines, hotels, car rentals and for tracking fares.

Fodor's Guide—www.fodors.com
The main search areas include a worldwide listing of hotels and restaurants. The site also includes miscellaneous related travel tips and information, and offers information featured in their guides and worldwide travel tips.

Global Online Travel—www.got.com/index.html
Provides links to worldwide vacation sites and real-time airline flight schedules and fares.

The Hotel Guide—www.hotelguide.com
Claims to be the world's largest Internet directory of hotels, both domestic and international. This guide lists over 60,000 hotels around the world, including accommodations of all types and all levels of luxury. You can search their database to check daily rates, facilities, and more. This site also provides the opportunity to book directly and save money!

QuickAID—www.quickaid.com
Provides links to airport directory information, toll-free telephone directory of travel businesses and links to other travel sites.

Sabre Interactive Travelocity—www.travelocity.com
Run by the parent company of American Airlines, this site offers extensive travel resources.

The Trip—www.thetrip.com
Touted as the preeminent site for the business traveler. One feature allows for real-time flight tracking.

Travel Channel Online Network—www.travelchannel.com
The Travel Channel's homepage. Offers featured travel topics, their television programming schedule, links to chats and forums, and links to other travel sites.

Travel Now—www.travelnow.com
Advertised as a source for booking your reservations online

with savings of up to 40% off. Lists approximately 20,000 hotels in 5,000 cities worldwide.

TravelGuide—www.touristguide.com
Listed as the premiere online source for recreation and business travelers.

Travelocity—www.travelocity.com
The main categories are Travel Reservations, Destinations & Interests, Chats & Forums, and Travel Merchandise.

Traveloco—www.traveloco.com
Virtual travel site providing features to out-of-the-way locations.

Travelon—www.travelon.com
Commercial site promoting its adventure and specialty vacations.

TravelSource—www.travelsource.com
This site is touted as being the Internet's "First Interactive Travel Guide." Its emphasis is on unique travel destinations and adventure vacations.

Xplore Travel—www.xplore.com/xplore500/medium/travel.html
Provides links to top travel sites.

Specific Information for Major Cities Worldwide

City Net—www.city.net
Provides links to major metropolitan areas. A search engine

allows searches by destination, subject, or address. Features lists of top U.S. and international cities.

BED AND BREAKFAST SITES

Bed & Breakfast Inns Online—www.bbonline.com
Provides independent reviews of over 700 Bed and Breakfast Inns worldwide, recipe and cookbook listings, and links to State Innkeepers Association web sites.

Tourist Guides: The Ultimate Bed & Breakfast Directory—www.innformation.com
Advertised as the largest and most complete B & B directory available.

CRUISE LINES AND FERRIES

Upscale Travel-Tours-Cruises—www.upscaletours.com
Providing personalized travel service for the sophisticated traveler looking for luxury tours and cruises to exciting destinations throughout the world.

CruiseWeb—www.cruiseweb.com
Provides listing to cruises on all CLIA member lines.

Ferry Travel Guide—www.youra.com/ferry
Provides national and international and public and private listing of ferry schedules. Also, offers links to cruise lines, shipping lines and other sites with ferry information.

IMPORTANT TRAVEL AGENCIES

The following agencies can provide excellent assistance for all types of travel problems.

American Passport Express—www.americanpassport.com
Provides information on obtaining and-or renewing American passports and additional passport information.

Centers for Disease Control Travel Information—www.cdc.gov
Provides a variety of health information for the international traveler.

Corporate Rate Hotel Directory— www. idt.net/corp_hotels
A site where you can look up the corporate rate of a hotel before making a reservation.

Shoreland's Travel Health Online— www.tripprep.com
Offers health and medical information for individuals traveling abroad.

U.S. Customs Service— www.customs.ustreas.gov
Provides an array of information for the traveler regarding U.S. Customs laws and regulations.

U.S. State Department Bureau of Consular Affairs—
www.travel.state.gov
Services provided include travel warnings, services and information for Americans abroad, travel publications, passport and visa information, judicial assistance, and a list of U.S. Embassy and consulate websites worldwide.

United States Embassies and Consulates Worldwide—
http://travel.state.gov/links.html
Visit the U.S. Embassy and Consulate home pages, to research any information regarding your travels.

Travel Software Tools

OAG Electronic Edition

A high-tech version of the resource frequent flyers have relied on for years. Accessible from any telecommunications terminal or personal computer, the OAG Electronic Edition brings on-screen to frequent flyers the latest airline schedules, fare and seat availability, and hotel information. In addition, you'll find databases with flight arrival and departure information, weather forecasts, and the most recent edition of InsideFlyer, (the most up-to-date information on how to maximize the miles and points you've already accrued, and get the most from bonus offers from airline, hotel, and car rental programs). The OAG Electronic Edition is available directly from OAG Travel Services or through many online services, including CompuServe, Dow Jones News-Retrieval, Dialcom, Dialog, Genie, and Western Union.

RATES: 47¢ per minute for prime-time usage; 17¢ per minute for off-hours usage when accessed directly from OAG. No-obligation 15-day free trial available.

PHONE ORDERS: Call 800-323-3537 for password and subscription information.

SOFTWARE PROGRAMS FOR TRAVELERS

AirEase

Combines the convenience of using the Web with a software component. Allows the users to compare their mileage statements to what they have tracked. Additionally, users can download the latest frequent flier news to make sure they are earning all available bonus miles.

COST: Version 1 can be downloaded for free. Version 2 will cost between $25–50.

WEB SITE: http://airease.net

MaxMiles Frequent Flyer Software

Tracking and planning software that makes it easy to record and reconcile your frequent flyer miles.

Software cost: $39

MAIL ORDERS:

MaxMiles Fulfillment Center
440 North Wells, Suite 600
Chicago, IL 60610

PHONE: 312 494-0394

WEB SITE: www:maxmiles.com

MileageMiner

This software is from the same company as MaxMiles. However, it requires no data entry. The service covers 25 airlines and hotel programs. Users receive one consolidated activity report, which can be viewed 24 hours a day. This site also contains the latest frequent-flier program information, supplied by *InsideFlyer* Magazine.

COST: $2.95 per month or $29.95 a year.

MAIL ORDERS:

MaxMiles Fulfillment Center
440 North Wells, Suite 600
Chicago, IL 60610

PHONE: 312 494-0394

WEB SITE: www:maxmiles.com/itn

Professional Traveler by TravelWare

A comprehensive software package for managing multiple frequent traveler accounts. Program features account management, trip itineraries, base and bonus mileage tracking, as well as displaying the amount of miles or points necessary to obtain a specific award. Professional Traveler will import travel activity from an airline reservation system, automatically calculate miles (both minimum mileage and bonus miles), keep track of an unlimited number of travelers' program accounts, and their respective award certificates. This software also offers award and program information for most frequent traveler programs plus a comparative award search. An IBM Windows-based system, Professional Traveler is compatible with most networks. This program is specifically designed to help corporate travel departments or travel agencies.

COST: Call for specific quote based on user requirements.

MAIL ORDERS:

TravelWare
2964 West 4700 South, Ste. 202
Salt Lake City, UT 84118

PHONE ORDERS: 801 965-1800, ext.30

FAX ORDERS: 801 965-6000

Additional Services

Frequent Flyer Club

Taking the services offered by frequent travel programs a giant step farther is the Frequent Flyer Club (FFC), an innovative program with several one-of-a-kind "member-only" benefits. Two levels of membership are available: Diamond Level for those frequent flyers who manage their own programs and want to stay well informed. These members receive a one-year subscription to InsideFlyer, a copy of The Official Frequent Flyer Guidebook, access to WebFlyer information service, a toll-free helpline, assistance with missing credit, and help with award travel planning; or Platinum Level for travelers who prefer professional management of their frequent travel program memberships. Benefits include those listed for Diamond

Level members plus advance notice of award expiration, and enrollment in AwardGuard which protects unused, accumulated points and miles if an airline or hotel company ceases operations because of financial default.

U.S. MEMBERSHIP RATES: $99 a year for Diamond Level; $124 a year for Platinum Level

OUTSIDE U.S. MEMBERSHIP RATES: $114 U.S. a year for Diamond International; $139 U.S. a year for Platinum International

MAIL ORDERS:

Frequent Flyer Club
4715-C Town Center Drive
Colorado Springs, CO 80916-4709

PHONE ORDERS: 800 333-5937 or 719 597-8843

FAX ORDERS: 719 597-6855

PrivilegeFlyer

A "must-have" for frequent flyers who want to get the most from their frequent traveler programs worldwide. Membership brings one-of-a-kind information sources, services, and protection that no savvy frequent flyer should be without. Membership in AwardGuard or AwardExtender includes a subscription to the monthly magazine InsideFlyer, a copy of the Official Frequent Flyer Guidebook, toll-free member helpline, automated telephone hotline, custom information via fax, plus substantial discounts on hotels, resorts, and car rentals. Extended benefits offer award protection for selected airline, hotel, car rental, and credit card award programs. Specifically, AwardGuard protects frequent traveler miles and points should an awards program fold because of financial default, and AwardExtender prolongs the life of expiring awards. Benefits also include default or bumped ticket protection, and award travel flight insurance.

RATES: PrivilegeFlyer—$79 a year, or $125 for two years
AwardGuard—$99 a year, $165 for 2 years
AwardExtender—$139 a year, $245 for 2 years
AwardWaiver—$10 a year
AwardGuard with AwardExtender—$159 a year

MAIL ORDERS:
PrivilegeFlyer
4715-C Town Center Drive
Colorado Springs, CO 80916-4709

PHONE ORDERS: 800 487-8893 or 719 597-8893

FAX ORDERS: 719 597-6855

Award Donation Center

If you have miles or awards that will expire soon or go unused, why not pass them on to an organization that will put them to good use? For more information on donating awards to non-profit organizations such as Big Brothers and Big Sisters of America or the Ronald McDonald Children's Charities, contact your airline for ways to donate.

Expert Sources

GETTING IN TOUCH WITH AIRLINE WATCHDOGS

To find out more about different airlines, lodge a complaint, or educate yourself about passenger rights, consider these organizations:

American Society of Travel Agents

A travel trade organization, ASTA represents some 23,000 airlines, hotels, travel agents, rental car agencies, and other travel businesses around the world. Their consumer office can provide info about packing or preparing to travel abroad and also can informally mediate consumer disputes with ASTA members. 703 739-2782

Aviation Consumer Action Project

Founded in 1971 by Ralph Nader, ACAP researches consumer issues and publishes the brochure "Facts and Advice for Airline Passengers." The group will advise you about passenger rights and safety issues over the phone. 202 638-4000

Federal Aviation Administration

CONSUMER HOTLINE: An FAA watchdog, the hotline is for complaints about problems with airport security, carry-on baggage, or the FAA itself. 800 322-7873

SAFETY HOTLINE: To report violations of federal airport and airplane regulation or unsafe situations. This is often the first stop for insider whistle-blowers. 800 255-1111

International Airline Passengers Association

Like members of the American Automobile Association, IAPA's 150,000 members can buy travel accident insurance or participate in the lost luggage retrieval assistance program. Their bimonthly travel-safety alert is a good resource for international travelers worried about airline safety and other travel problems. 214 404-9980

U.S. Department of Transportation

Consumer and Community Affairs Office: Specializes in problems with baggage handling, overbooking, and delayed flights. Also releases monthly statistics based on consumer complaints and airline reports. 202 366-2220

Directory of Travel Companies

MAJOR DOMESTIC AIRLINES

AIRLINE	TOLL-FREE NUMBER	WEB SITE
Alaska Air	800 426-0333	www.alaska-air.com
Aloha Air	800 367-5250	www.alohaair.com-aloha-air
America West Airlines	800 235-9292	www.americawest.com
American Airlines	800 433-7300	www.AA.com
Carnival Airlines	800 824-7386	www.carnivalair.com
Comair—The Delta Connection	800 354-9822	http://fly-comair.com
Continental Airlines	800 525-0280	www.flycontinental.com
Delta Air Lines	800 221-1212	www.delta-air.com
Hawaiian Airlines	800 367-5320	www.hawaiianair.com
Midwest Express	800 452-2022	www.midwestexpress.com
Northwest Airlines	800 225-2525	www.nwa.com
Reno Air	800 736-6247	www.renoair.com
Skywest Airlines	800 453-9417	www.skywest-air.com
Southwest Airlines	800 435-9792	www.iflyswa.com
Tower Air	800 221-2500	www.towerair.com
TWA	800 221-2000	www.twa.com
United Airlines	800 241-6522	www.ual.com
US Airways	800 428-4322	www.usairways.com
Western Pacific Airlines	800 930-3030	www.westpac.com
WestJet Airlines	800 538-5696	www.westjet.com
World Airways	800 967-5350	www.worldair.com

INTERNATIONAL AIRLINES

AIRLINE	TOLL-FREE NUMBER	WEB SITE
Aer Lingus	800 223-6537	www.aerlingus.ie
Aero Costa Rica	800 237-6274	www.centralamerica.com
Aeromexico	800 237-6639	www.wotw.com-aeromexico
Air Canada	800 776-3000	www.aircanada.ca
Air China	800 986-1985	www.airchina.com
Air France	800 237-2747	www.airfrance.fr
Air New Zealand	800 262-1234	www.airnz.com
Air Pacific	800 227-4446	www.fijifvb.gov.fj/airlines/ airpac.htm
Air UK	800 249-2478	www.airuk.co.uk
Alitalia	800 223-5730	www.alitalia.it
All Nippon Airways	800 235-9262	www.ana.co.jp
Ansett Airlines	800 366-1300	www.ansett.com
Asiana Airlines	800 227-4262	www.kumho.co
Austrian Airlines	800 843-0002	www.aua.at/aua
Aviateca Guatemala	800 535-4148	www.grupotaca.com
British Airways	800 247-9297	www.british-airways.com
British Midland	800 788-0555	www.iflybritishmidland.com
Canadian Airlines	800 426-7000	www.cdnair.ca
Cathay Pacific	800 233-2742	www.cathay-usa.com
China Airlines	800 227-5118	www.china-airlines.com
Condor	800 524-6975	www.condor.de
Cyprus Airways	800 333-2977	www.cyprusair.com
Czech Airlines	800 223-2365	www.csa.cz
El AL Israel Airlines	800 223-6700	www.elal.co.il

AIRLINE	TOLL-FREE NUMBER	WEB SITE
Emirates	800 777-3999	www.ekgroup.com
Garuda Indonesia	800 432-1359	www.aerowisata.com/garuda/index.html
Iberia	800 772-4642	www.iberia.com
Iceland Air	800 223-5500	www.icelandair.is
Japan Airlines	800 525-3663	www.jal.co.jp
Kenya Airways	800 343-2506	n/a
KLM—Royal Dutch Airlines	800 374-7747	www.klm.nl
Korean Air	800 438-5000	www.koreanair.com
Lan-Chile Airlines	800 735-5526	www.lanchile.com
Lauda Air	800 645-3880	www.laudaair.com
Lufthansa	800 645-3880	www.lufthansa.com
Malaysia Airlines	800 421-8641	www.malaysia-airlines.com
Malev Hungarian Airlines	800 223-6884	www.malev.hu
Mexicana	800 531-7921	www.mexicana.com
Pakistan International Airlines	800 221-2552	www.piac.com
Philippine Airlines	800 435-9725	www.pal.com.ph
Polish Air-Lot	800 223-0593	www.lot.com
Polynesian Airlines	800 677-4277	www.pacificislands.com/ailines/polynesian.html
Qantas	800 227-4500	www.qantas.com.au
Royal Air Maroc	800 344-6726	www.kingdomoforocco.com
Royal Jordanian	800 223-0470	www.rja.com.jo
Royal Nepal Airlines	800 266-3725	www.adventurecenter.com/ra.htm
Sabena	800 955-2000	www.sabena.com
SAS	800 221-2350	www.sas.se
Saudia	800 472-8342	www.saudiairblanairlines.com

AIRLINE	TOLL-FREE NUMBER	WEB SITE
Singapore Airlines	800 742-3333	www.singaporeair.com
South African Airways	800 722-9675	www.saa.co.za/saa
Swissair	800 221-4750	www.swissair.com
Taesa—Airline serving Mexico	800 848-2372	www.taesa.com.mx
TAP Air Portugal	800 221-7370	www.tap.pt/en
Thai Airways	800 221-7370	www.thaiairways.com
Tower Air	800 221-2500	www.towerair.com
Transbrasil	800 872-3153	www.transbrasil.com.br
Turkish Airlines	800 874-8875	www.turkishairlines.com
Varig	800 468-2744	www.varig.com.br
VASP	800 433-0444	www.vasp.com.
Virgin Atlantic Airways	800 862-8621	www.fly.virgin.com
Zimbabwe Express Airlines	800 223-1136	http:—rapidttp.com

SELECTED HOTEL CHAINS

With over 35,000 hotels to chose from it would be unfeasible to list every hotel. Therefore, I have limited my list of hotels to those that in my opinion provide excellent service and value for the money. Additional hotels can be found with the *Small Hotels of the World Directory*, *The Leading Hotels of the World, the Hotel Guide, American Express Platinum Guide Book* and by using one of the many internet sites listed.

LUXURY HOTELS	RATE RANGE	AVG. RATE	FREQUENT GUEST PROGRAM	WEB SITE
Four Seasons 800 332-3442	$125–225	$175	Unofficial tracking of stays	www.fourseasons.com
Ritz-Carlton 800 241-3333	$150–225	$180	Unofficial tracking of stays	www.ritzcarlton.com
Hyatt Hotels 800 233-1234	$100–150	$120	Gold Passport 800 492-8891	www.hyatt.com

Source: Consumer Reports Online, June 1998

UPSCALE HOTELS	RATE RANGE	AVG. RATE	FREQUENT GUEST PROGRAM	WEB SITE
Adam's Mark 800 444-2326	$80–$100	$90	Gold Mark Club	http://www.adams-mark.com
Crowne Plaza 800 227-6963	$83–115	$98	Priority Club 800 777-9273	www.crowneplaza.com
Disney Resorts 714 956-6425 (CA) 407 934-7639 (FL)	$110–187	$140	None	www.disney.com
Doubletree Hotels 800 222-8733	$81–115	$99	None	www.double-treehotels.com
Embassy Suites 800 362-2779	$90–120	$100	None	www.embassysuites.com
Harrah's 800 427-7247	$45–85	$60	None	Varies by hotel

UPSCALE HOTELS	RATE RANGE	AVG. RATE	FREQUENT GUEST PROGRAM	WEB SITE
Hilton 800 544-3197	$84–125	$100	Hilton Honors 972 788-0878	www.hilton.com
Inter-Continental Hotels 800 442-7375	$120–175	$150	Six Continent Club 800 462-6686	www.interconti.com
Marriott 800 627-7468	$89–125	$100	Marriott Rewards 800 450-4442	www.marriott.com
Omni 800 843-6664	$90–125	$105	Select Guest 877 440-6664	www.omnihotels.com
Radisson 800 333-3333	$75–100	$89	Individual hotels track status	www.radisson.com
Renaissance Hotels 800 468-3571	$99–150	$120	Marriott Rewards 800 450-4442	www.renaissance-hotels.com
Sheraton 800 325-3535	$84–125	$100	Sheraton Club 800 247-2582	www.sheraton.com
Westin Hotels 800 228-3000	$102–150	$125	Westin Premier 800 521-2000	www.westin.com
Wyndham 800 996-3426	$80–120	$99	Individual hotels have own programs	Varies by hotel

Source: Consumer Reports Online, June 1998

SELECT INDIVIDUAL HOTELS

Claridge, London	44-171-629-8860	One of London's most splendid hotels, serving distinguished guests for almost 100 years.
Hotel Bel-Air, Los Angeles	310 472-1211	An intimate retreat nestled in the famed residential district of Bel-Air.
Hotel George V, Paris	47-23-54-00	Charming, stately, in the heart of Paris
Hotel Ritz, Paris	33-1-43-16-30-30	The pinnacle of refinement in every detail from opulent fabrics to breathtaking floral displays.
Lodge at Koele, Lanai Hawaii	808 565-7300	Secluded and tranquil, offering an excellent environment for relaxation and challenging golf.
Mandarin Oriental, Hong Kong	852-2522-0111	Subtle opulence and attentive service has made this hotel a legend.
Peaks at Telluride, CO	970 728-6800	Offers a unique western experience with quaint Victorian charm.
Raffles Hotel, Singapore	65-337-1886	Elegant property offering high molded ceilings and polished teak. Each suite is appointed with period furnishings.
Ritz-Carlton Bali	62-361-702-222	Exquisite service on a magical island.
Ritz-Carlton Kapalua, Maui	808 669-6200	Refined elegance in paradise. My top resort!
The Carlyle, New York	212 744-1600	Five Star quality for over a quarter of a century.
The Oriental, Bangkok	66-2-236-0400	Uniquely seated on the bank of the Chao Phya River, offering skilled yet unobtrusive service.
The Savoy, London	44-171-836-4343	One of the world's most glamorous hotels, offering breathtaking views of the Thames.
The St. Regis, New York	212 753-4500	Turn of the century elegance.
Windsor Court, New Orleans	504 596-4513	Understated elegance steps from the French Quarter. My top choice of hotels.

Car Rental Companies

Alamo Rent A Car	800 327-9633	www.freeways.com
Avis Rent A Car	800 831-2847	www.avis.com
Budget Rent A Car	800 527-0700	www.budgetrentacar.com
Dollar Rent A Car	800 800-4000	www.dollarcar.com
Enterprise Rent A Car	800 325-8007	www.pickenterprise.com
Hertz Rent A Car	800 654-3131	www.hertz.com
National Rent A Car	800 227-7368	www.nationalcar.com
Payless Car Rental	800 729-5377	www.800payless.com
Rent A Wreck	800 535-1391	www.rent-a-wreck.com
Thrifty Car Rental	800 367-2277	www.thrifty.com

Credit Card Programs That Can Earn You Points for Upgrades and Discounts

American Express Membership Rewards	800 297-3276	www.americanexpress.com
Diners Club Club Rewards	800 234-6377	www.dinnerculb.com
American Airlines Advantage—Citibank	800 843-0777	www.citibank.com
United Airlines Mileage Plus—First Card	800 537-7783	www.fcnbd.com
Continental One Pass—Chase Bank	800 323-6252	www.chase.com
USAir—Nations Bank	800 241-6295	www.nationsbank.com
Northwest Worldperks—First Bank System	800 285-8585	www.usbank.com
American Express Skymiles	800 843-2273	www.americanexpress.com
American Express Hilton Optima	800 843-2273	www.americanexpress.com

Frequent Flyer Programs

QUALIFYING FOR ELITE STATUS ON MAJOR DOMESTIC AIRLINES

AIRLINE	NAME OF PROGRAM	REQUIREMENTS FOR ELITE STATUS	MILEAGE BONUS	COMPLIMENTARY UPGRADES	ELIGIBLE FARES FOR UPGRADES	WHEN TO CONFIRM UPGRADE
Alaska Mileage Plan 800 654-5669	MVP	15,000 base miles	50%	Every 10,000 miles flown	All	Time of booking
	MVP Gold[1]	45,000 base miles	100%	Every 5,000 miles flown	All	Time of booking
American Advantage 800 882-8880	Gold	25,000 base miles	25%	Every 10,000 miles flown	All	24 hours prior to departure
	Platinum	50,000 base miles	100%	Every 10,000 miles flown	All	72 hours prior to departure
	Executive Platinum	100,000 points[2]	100%	Every 10,000 miles flown	All	100 hours prior to departure
America West 800 247-5691	Chairman Club	20,000 base miles	50%	Every 10,000 miles flown	All	Full fare: at time of ticketing. All other fares: 72 hours prior to departure
	Chairman Club Masters	50,000 base miles	100%	Every 10,000 miles flown	All	Full fare: at time of ticketing. All other fares: 72 hours prior to departure
Continental Onepass[3] 713 952-1630	Silver	25,000 base miles or 30 flight segments	50%	Unlimited	All	Full fare 48 hours prior to departure. All other fares: day of departure

AIRLINE	NAME OF PROGRAM	REQUIRE-MENTS FOR ELITE STATUS	MILEAGE BONUS	COMPLIMENTARY UPGRADES	ELIGIBLE FARES FOR UPGRADES	WHEN TO CONFIRM UPGRADE
	Gold	50,000 base miles or 60 flight segments	100%	Unlimited	All	Full fare: at time of ticketing. All other fares: 48 hours prior to departure
	Platinum	100,000 base miles or 90 flight segments	125%	Unlimited	All	Full fare: at time of ticketing. All other fares: 72 hours prior to departure
Delta Skymiles 800 323-2323	Medallion	25,000 base miles or 30 flight segments	25%	Every 10,000 miles flown	All fares expect L-class	24 hours prior to departure
	Gold Medallion	50,000 base miles or 60 flight segments	100%	Every 10,000 miles flown	All fares except L-class	72 hours prior to departure
	Platinum Medallion[4]	100,000 base miles or 100 flight segments	100%	Unlimited	All fares except L-class	Time of booking
Northwest Worldperks[5] 800 447-3757	Silver Elite	25,000 base miles	50%	Unlimited	All	Full fare: any time. All other fares: day of departure
	Gold Elite	50,000 base miles	100%	Unlimited	All	Full fare: any time. All other fares: 48 hours prior to departure
	Platinum Elite	75,000 base miles	125%	Unlimited	All	Full fare: any time. All other fares: 72 hours prior to departure

AIRLINE	NAME OF PROGRAM	REQUIRE-MENTS FOR ELITE STATUS	MILEAGE BONUS	COMPLIMENTARY UPGRADES	ELIGIBLE FARES FOR UPGRADES	WHEN TO CONFIRM UPGRADE
TWA Aviators 800 325-4815	Elite	20,000 base miles or $5000 in paid air tickets	25%	Full fare: every 5,000 miles flown. All other fares: every 10,000 miles . flown		Full fare: 48 hours prior to departure. All other fares: 24 hours prior to departure.
	Elite I	40,000 base miles or $10,000 in paid air tickets	50%	Full fare: every 3,000 miles flown. All other fares: every 7,000 miles flown.		Full fare: at time of booking. All other fares: 72 hours prior to departure.
	Platinum	100,000 base miles or $20,000 in paid air tickets	100%	Unlimited		Full fare: at time of booking. All other fares: 100 hours prior to departure
US Airways 800 872-4738	Preferred	25,000 base miles	25%	Every 10,000 miles flown	All	24 hours prior to departure
	Preferred Plus	50,000 base miles	100%	Every 10,000 miles flown	All	72 hours prior to departure
	Chairman Preferred[6]	100,000 base miles	100%	Unlimited	All	
United Mileage Plus 605 399-2400	Premier	25,000 base miles or 30 flight segments	25%	Every 10,000 miles flown	All	Full fare: 72 hours prior to departure. All other fares: 24 hours prior to departure
	Premier Executive	50,000 base miles or 60 flight segments	25%	Every 10,000 miles flown	All	All fares: 72 hours prior to departure

AIRLINE	NAME OF PROGRAM	REQUIRE-MENTS FOR ELITE STATUS	MILEAGE BONUS	COMPLIMENTARY UPGRADES	ELIGIBLE FARES FOR UPGRADES	WHEN TO CONFIRM UPGRADE
United (cont.)	100K	100,000 base miles	100%	Every 10,000 miles flown	All	All fares: 100 hours prior to departure

Information accurate as of 12/98

[1] Boardroom initiation fee is waived
[2] Points based on fare paid: First Class=1.5 points per miles flown; Business Class=1.25 points per miles flown; full-fare Economy=1.0 points per miles flown; any discounted coach fare = .05 points per miles flown
[3] Can earn base miles for flights on Northwest Airlines
[4] Includes Annual Crown Room Membership
[5] Can earn base miles for flights on Continental Airlines
[6] Complimentary membership in the US Airways Club

Mileage Award Requirements

The following charts summarize how you can fly in either business or first class on most major domestic carriers by using your frequent flyer program, either through mileage upgrades or purchasing upgrades (available on domestic/North America flights only). Please note that each frequent flyer program has additional benefits and upgrade possibilities other than those noted below, so be sure to obtain a benefit handbook and read the fine print thoroughly.

NOTE: Peak season and Non-Peak season varies by airline and destination. Alaska and Northwest are the primary domestic carriers that use this designation.

NORTH AMERICA

AIRLINE	FF MILE EXCHANGE FOR UPGRADES	PURCHASING UPGRADES	FREE BUSINESS CLASS TICKET USING FF MILES	FREE FIRST CLASS TICKET USING FF MILES
Alaska Air	5000– Elite Members; 10000– All others	$40 per 1250 miles of flight	N/A	40000– Non Peak Season; 60000– Peak Season
American	15000– Full fare 20000– Rest. fare	N/A	N/A	40000– Restricted 80000– Non-Restricted
America West	20000	$60 per 500 miles of flight Elite–any fare Non-Elite– Full Fare	N/A	45000
Continental	10000 OW 20000 RT	N/A	N/A	45000
Delta	5000 OW Full Fare 10000 OW Rest. Fare	$40 per 500 miles of flight	N/A	40000
Northwest	5000 OW Full Fare Non peak; 10000 OW Rest. Fare Non Peak; 10000 OW Full Fare Rest. Availability; 20000 OW Rest. Fare Rest. Availability	N/A	N/A	40000 Non-Restricted 45000 Rest. Availability
TWA	10000 Full Fare 20000 Rest. Fare	N/A	N/A	40000 Rest. Availability 80000 Non-Restricted

AIRLINE	FF MILE EXCHANGE FOR UPGRADES	PURCHASING UPGRADES	FREE BUSINESS CLASS TICKET USING FF MILES	FREE FIRST CLASS TICKET USING FF MILES
US Airways	2500— 0–799 miles OW; 5000— 800–1799 miles OW; 7500— 1800 + miles OW Full Fare only	$400 per 11 coupons[1] Full Fare only	N/A	40000
United	10000 RT Full Fare; 20000 RT Rest. Fare	$40 per 500 miles; $25 per 500 miles —Elite	40000 Rest. Availability; 80000 Non-Restricted	60000 Rest. Availability; 120000 Non-Restricted

Information accurate as of 12/98

[1] One coupon = 0–799 miles; Two coupons = 800–1799 miles; Three coupons = 1800+ miles

KEY:
OW = One Way
RT = Round Trip

HAWAII

AIRLINE	FF MILE EXCHANGE FOR UPGRADES	FREE BUSINESS CLASS TICKET USING FF MILES	FREE FIRST CLASS TICKET USING FF MILES
Alaska Air	N/A	N/A	60000
American	15000 OW 30000 RT	N/A	60000 Rest. Availability 120000 Non-Restricted
America West*	N/A	60000	60000
Continental	20000 OW 40000 RT	60000	60000
Delta	75000 OW Full Fare 15000 OW Rest. Fare	N/A	60000
Northwest	7500 OW Non Peak 17500 OW Rest. Availability	N/A	60000
TWA	15000 Rest. Fare 30000 Full Fare	N/A	60000 Rest. Availability 20000 Non-Restricted
US Airways	N/A	N/A	N/A
United	15000 Full Fare RT 30000 Rest. Fare RT	60000 Rest. Availability 120000 Non-Restricted	80000 Rest. Availability 160000 Non-Restricted

*Flights occur on alliance partner or code share carrier.

EUROPE

AIRLINE	FF MILE EXCHANGE FOR UPGRADES	FREE BUSINESS CLASS TICKET USING FF MILES	FREE FIRST CLASS TICKET USING FF MI
Alaska Air	N/A	80000*	85000* 100000*
American	25000 OW 40000 RT	80000 Rest. Availability 160000 Non-Restricted	100000 Rest. Availability 200000 Non-Restricted
America West*	60000	100000	100000
Continental	20000 40000	100000	N/A
Delta	40000 RT	N/A	80000
Northwest	20000 Non Peak 40000 Rest. Availability	80000	100000
TWA	20000 Full Fare 40000 Rest. Fare	N/A	80000 Rest. Availability 160000 Non-Restricted
US Airways	N/A	80000	100000*
United	20000 RT Full Fare 40000 RT Rest Fare	80000 Rest. Availability 150000 Non-Restricted	100000 Rest. Availability 200000 Non-Restricted

*Flights occur on alliance partner or code share carrier.

ASIA

AIRLINE	FF MILE EXCHANGE FOR UPGRADES	FREE BUSINESS CLASS TICKET USING FF MILES	FREE FIRST CLASS TICKET USING FF MILES
Alaska Air	N/A	90000	120000
American	15000 Full Fare OW 25000 Full Fare 40000 Rest. Fare	90000 Rest. Availability 180000 Non-Restricted	120000 Rest. Availability 240000 Non-Restricted
America West*	N/A	120000	120000
Continental	25000 50000	100000	N/A
Delta	50000	N/A	90000
Northwest	12500 OW Full Fare 25000 OW Rest. Fare	75000 Non-Peak 90000 Peak	100000 Non-Peak Season 120000 Peak Season
TWA	N/A	N/A	N/A
US Airways*	N/A	90000	120000
United	25000 Full Fare RT 50000 Rest. Fare RT	90000 Rest. Availability 150000 Non-Restricted	120000 Rest. Availability 200000 Non-Restricted

*Flights occur on alliance partner or code share carrier.

AUSTRALIA/NEW ZEALAND/SOUTH PACIFIC

AIRLINE	FF MILE EXCHANGE FOR UPGRADES	FREE BUSINESS CLASS TICKET USING FF MILES	FREE FIRST CLASS TICKET USING FF MILES
Alaska Air*	N/A	N/A	N/A
American*	25000 Full Fare Coach to Business Class 50000 Business Class to First Class	105000	135000
America= West	N/A	N/A	N/A
Continental	N/A	N/A	N/A
Delta	N/A	N/A	N/A
Northwest	N/A	N/A	N/A
TWA	N/A	N/A	N/A
US Airways[2]	N/A	95000	125000
United	25000 Full Fare RT 50000 Rest. Fare RT	90000 Rest. Availability 150000 Non-Restricted	120000 Rest. Availability 200000 Non-Restricted

*Flights occur on alliance partner or code share carrier.

[2]From Business Class to First Class

AROUND THE WORLD

AIRLINE	FF MILE EXCHANGE FOR UPGRADES	FREE BUSINESS CLASS TICKET USING FF MILES	FREE FIRST CLASS TICKET USING FF MILES
Alaska Air	N/A	N/A	N/A
American	N/A	N/A	N/A
America West	N/A	N/A	N/A
Continental	N/A	N/A	N/A
Delta	N/A	N/A	310000
Northwest	N/A	325000	350000
TWA	N/A	N/A	400000
US Airways	N/A	N/A	N/A
United	N/A	N/A	240000 Rest. Availability 480000 Non-Restricted

Which Airline Awards the Most Seats?

American	1,084,343	8.5%	+2.9%
United	1,026,526	6.6	+5.2
Delta	646,671	5.4	-20.5
Continental	551,041	7.2	-2.4
Northwest	466,397	7.8	+8.6
US Airways	356,788	6.6	-17.2
TWA	214,547	8.5	-6.1
Total	**4,346,313**	**7.0**	**-3.4**

Compared with fiscal year 1996.
Source: 1997 DOT data; GRA Inc.; Consumer Reports

Index

Acknowledgements

The journey of this book owes its indebtedness to many. A special thanks to the many travelers whom I met on the endless road, for all that I learned from their stories and insightful tips. A most warm and deep appreciation for my agent, Patricia Snell, whose belief and dedication to this project is largely responsible for its reality today. My gratitude is passed along to James O'Reilly and Larry Habegger for their guidance through the publishing of this book. Thanks to Susan Brady for graciously dealing with my many calls and manuscript changes. I wish to recognize the entire staff at Travelers' Tales for their invaluable assistance. Special thanks to Diane Mitchell for helping to launch this book. A profound and heartfelt acknowledgement to Laurie Viera, whose dedication, intensity, and willingness to become intimately involved with this book is the undeviating reason for what it has become. Without her precise editing skills it would merely be a cluster of the alphabet. Lastly, I am grateful to my wife Nancy for her support through the writing of this book.

About the Author

Joel Widzer's travels have taken him to more than 20 countries, logging over 100,000 air miles a year and accumulating more than 1.5 million frequent flyer miles. He has developed the unique ability to approach travel from the point of view of a consumer as well as from a business perspective. His pursuit of luxury travel while maintaining loyalty earned him the coveted Million-Miler award from Delta Airlines and invitations to participate in Delta's frequent flyer's round table discussions.

He has a Bachelor of Science degree in Business Administration from Pepperdine University and has pursued a career in sales and marketing. He has appeared as a motivational speaker to sales organizations and Fortune 500 companies nationwide.

In writing *The Penny Pincher's Passport to Luxury Travel,* Joel drew on his own travel experience and his extensive research of the travel industry. His intimate understanding of travel programs has allowed him to travel the world in ultimate luxury while paying coach prices, secrets he shares with readers.

Currently, Joel is completing a doctoral degree in Industrial/Organizational Psychology. He lives with his wife, Nancy, in Tustin Ranch, California, and has a nine-year-old daughter.

TRAVELERS' TALES GUIDES

LOOK FOR THESE TITLES IN THE SERIES

FOOTSTEPS: THE SOUL OF TRAVEL

A NEW IMPRINT FROM TRAVELERS' TALES GUIDES

An imprint of Travelers' Tales Guides, the Footsteps series unveils new works by first-time authors, established writers, and reprints of works whose time has come…again. Each book will fire your imagination, disturb your sleep, and feed your soul.

KITE STRINGS OF THE SOUTHERN CROSS
A Woman's Travel Odyssey
By Laurie Gough
ISBN 1-885211-30-9
400 pages, $24.00, Hardcover

THE SWORD OF HEAVEN
A Five Continent Odyssey to Save the World
By Mikkel Aaland
ISBN 1-885211-44-9
350 pages, $24.00, Hardcover

STORM
A Motorcycle Journey of Love, Endurance, and Transformation
By Allen Noren
ISBN 1-885211-45-7
360 pages, $24.00, Hardcover

SPECIAL INTEREST

THE FEARLESS SHOPPER:
How to Get the Best Deals on the Planet
By Kathy Borrus
ISBN 1-885211-39-2, 200 pages, $12.95

Special Interest

THE GIFT OF RIVERS:
True Stories of Life on the Water

Edited by Pamela Michael

Introduction by Robert Hass

ISBN 1-885211-42-2, 256 pages, $14.95

SHITTING PRETTY:
How to Stay Clean and Healthy While Traveling

By Dr. Jane Wilson-Howarth

ISBN 1-885211-47-3, 200 pages, $12.95

THE GIFT OF BIRDS:
True Encounters with Avian Spirits

Edited by Larry Habegger & Amy G. Carlson

ISBN 1-885211-41-4, 352 pages, $17.95

TESTOSTERONE PLANET:
True Stories from a Man's World

Edited by Sean O'Reilly, Larry Habegger & James O'Reilly

ISBN 1-885211-43-0, 300 pages, $17.95

THE PENNY PINCHER'S PASSPORT TO LUXURY TRAVEL:
The Art of Cultivating Preferred Customer Status

By Joel L. Widzer

ISBN 1-885211-31-7, 253 pages, $12.95

SPECIAL INTEREST

DANGER!
True Stories of Trouble and Survival
Edited by James O'Reilly, Larry Habegger & Sean O'Reilly
ISBN 1-885211-32-5, 336 pages, $17.95

FAMILY TRAVEL:
The Farther You Go, the Closer You Get
Edited by Laura Manske
ISBN 1-885211-33-3, 368 pages, $17.95

THE GIFT OF TRAVEL:
The Best of Travelers' Tales
Edited by Larry Habegger, James O'Reilly & Sean O'Reilly
ISBN 1-885211-25-2, 240 pages, $14.95

THERE'S NO TOILET PAPER...ON THE ROAD LESS TRAVELED:
The Best of Travel Humor and Misadventure
Edited by Doug Lansky
ISBN 1-885211-27-9, 207 pages, $12.95

A DOG'S WORLD:
True Stories of Man's Best Friend on the Road
Edited by Christine Hunsicker
ISBN 1-885211-23-6, 257 pages, $12.95

WOMEN'S TRAVEL

A WOMAN'S PATH:
Women's Best Spiritual Travel Writing
Edited by Lucy McCauley, Amy G. Carlson, and Jennifer Leo
ISBN 1-885211-48-1, 320 pages, $16.95

A WOMAN'S PASSION FOR TRAVEL:
More True Stories from A Woman's World
Edited by Marybeth Bond & Pamela Michael
ISBN 1-885211-36-8, 375 pages, $17.95

SAFETY AND SECURITY FOR WOMEN WHO TRAVEL
By Sheila Swan & Peter Laufer
ISBN 1-885211-29-5, 159 pages, $12.95

WOMEN IN THE WILD:
True Stories of Adventure and Connection
Edited by Lucy McCauley
ISBN 1-885211-21-X, 307 pages, $17.95

A MOTHER'S WORLD:
Journeys of the Heart
Edited by Marybeth Bond & Pamela Michael
ISBN 1-885211-26-0, 233 pages, $14.95

WOMEN'S TRAVEL

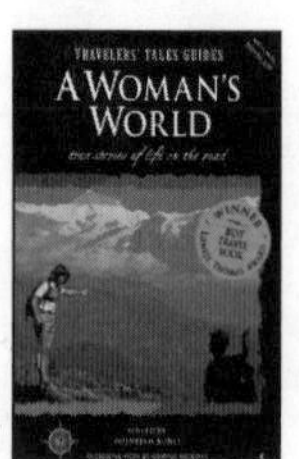

A WOMAN'S WORLD:
True Stories of Life on the Road
Edited by Marybeth Bond
Introduction by Dervla Murphy
ISBN 1-885211-06-6
475 pages, $17.95

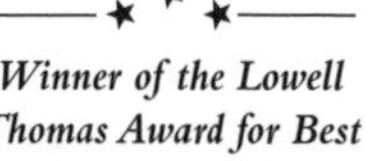

Winner of the Lowell Thomas Award for Best Travel Book—Society of American Travel Writers

GUTSY WOMEN:
Travel Tips and Wisdom for the Road
By Marybeth Bond
ISBN 1-885211-15-5, 123 pages, $7.95

GUTSY MAMAS:
Travel Tips and Wisdom for Mothers on the Road
By Marybeth Bond
ISBN 1-885211-20-1, 139 pages, $7.95

BODY & SOUL

THE ULTIMATE JOURNEY:
Inspiring Stories of Living and Dying
James O'Reilly, Larry Habegger & Richard Sterling
ISBN 1-885211-38-4
336 pages, $17.95

ADVENTURE OF FOOD:
True Stories of Eating Everything
Edited by Richard Sterling
ISBN 1-885211-37-6
336 pages, $17.95

BODY & SOUL

THE ROAD WITHIN:
True Stories of Transformation and the Soul
Edited by Sean O'Reilly, James O'Reilly & Tim O'Reilly
ISBN 1-885211-19-8, 459 pages, $17.95

★ ★ ★

Small Press Book Award Winner and Benjamin Franklin Award Finalist

LOVE & ROMANCE:
True Stories of Passion on the Road
Edited by Judith Babcock Wylie
ISBN 1-885211-18-X, 319 pages, $17.95

FOOD:
A Taste of the Road
Edited by Richard Sterling
Introduction by Margo True
ISBN 1-885211-09-0
467 pages, $17.95

★ ★ ★

Silver Medal Winner of the Lowell Thomas Award for Best Travel Book–Society of American Travel Writers

THE FEARLESS DINER:
Travel Tips and Wisdom for Eating around the World
By Richard Sterling
ISBN 1-885211-22-8, 139 pages, $7.95

COUNTRY GUIDES

IRELAND
True Stories of Life on the Emerald Isle
Edited by James O'Reilly, Larry Habegger, and Sean O'Reilly
ISBN 1-885211-46-5, 368 pages, $17.95

COUNTRY GUIDES

AUSTRALIA
True Stories of Life Down Under
Edited by Larry Habegger
ISBN 1-885211-40-6, 375 pages, $17.95

AMERICA
Edited by Fred Setterberg
ISBN 1-885211-28-7, 550 pages, $19.95

JAPAN
Edited by Donald W. George
& Amy Greimann Carlson
ISBN 1-885211-04-X, 437 pages, $17.95

ITALY
Edited by Anne Calcagno
Introduction by Jan Morris
ISBN 1-885211-16-3, 463 pages, $17.95

INDIA
Edited by James O'Reilly & Larry Habegger
ISBN 1-885211-01-5, 538 pages, $17.95

*C*OUNTRY GUIDES

FRANCE

Edited by James O'Reilly, Larry Habegger & Sean O'Reilly

ISBN 1-885211-02-3, 517 pages, $17.95

MEXICO

Edited by James O'Reilly & Larry Habegger

ISBN 1-885211-00-7, 463 pages, $17.95

THAILAND

Winner of the Lowell Thomas Award for Best Travel Book—Society of American Travel Writers

Edited by James O'Reilly & Larry Habegger

ISBN 1-885211-05-8

483 pages, $17.95

SPAIN

Edited by Lucy McCauley

ISBN 1-885211-07-4, 495 pages, $17.95

NEPAL

Edited by Rajendra S. Khadka

ISBN 1-885211-14-7, 423 pages, $17.95

*C*OUNTRY GUIDES

BRAZIL

Edited by Annette Haddad & Scott Doggett
Introduction by Alex Shoumatoff
ISBN 1-885211-11-2
452 pages, $17.95

—★ ★ ★—
Benjamin Franklin Award Winner

*C*ITY GUIDES

HONG KONG

Edited by James O'Reilly, Larry Habegger & Sean O'Reilly
ISBN 1-885211-03-1, 439 pages, $17.95

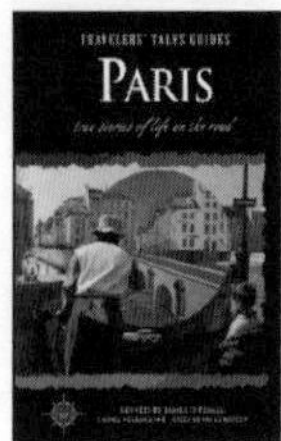

PARIS

Edited by James O'Reilly, Larry Habegger & Sean O'Reilly
ISBN 1-885211-10-4, 417 pages, $17.95

SAN FRANCISCO

Edited by James O'Reilly, Larry Habegger & Sean O'Reilly
ISBN 1-885211-08-2, 491 pages, $17.95

ℛEGIONAL GUIDES

HAWAI'I
True Stories of the Island Spirit
Edited by Rick & Marcie Carroll
ISBN 1-885211-35-X, 416 pages, $17.95

GRAND CANYON
True Stories of Life Below the Rim
Edited by Sean O'Reilly,
James O'Reilly & Larry Habegger
ISBN 1-885211-34-1, 296 pages, $17.95

SUBMIT YOUR OWN TRAVEL TALE

Do you have a tale of your own that you would like to submit to Travelers' Tales? We highly recommend that you first read one or more of our books to get a feel for the kind of story we're looking for. For submission guidelines and a list of titles in the works, send a SASE to:

Travelers' Tales Submission Guidelines
330 Townsend Street, Suite 208, San Francisco, CA 94107

or send email to ***guidelines@travelerstales.com***
or visit our Web site at **www.travelerstales.com**

You can send your story to the address above or via email to ***submit@travelerstales.com***. On the outside of the envelope, ***please indicate what country/topic your story is about***. If your story is selected for one of our titles, we will contact you about rights and payment.

We hope to hear from you. In the meantime, enjoy the stories!